Distributed Decision Making
Report of a Workshop

Committee on Human Factors
Commission on Behavioral and Social Sciences and Education
National Research Council

National Academy Press
Washington, D.C. 1990

NOTICE: The project that is the subject of this report was approved by the Governing Board of the National Research Council, whose members are drawn from the councils of the National Academy of Sciences, the National Academy of Engineering, and the Institute of Medicine. The members of the committee responsible for the report were chosen for their special competences and with regard to appropriate balance.

This report has been reviewed by a group other than the authors according to procedures approved by a Report Review Committee consisting of members of the National Academy of Sciences, the National Academy of Engineering, and the Institute of Medicine.

The National Academy of Sciences is a private, nonprofit, self-perpetuating society of distinguished scholars engaged in scientific and engineering research, dedicated to the furtherance of science and technology and to their use for the general welfare. Upon the authority of the charter granted to it by the Congress in 1863, the Academy has a mandate that requires it to advise the federal government on scientific and technical matters. Dr. Frank Press is president of the National Academy of Sciences.

The National Academy of Engineering was established in 1964, under the charter of the National Academy of Sciences, as a parallel organization of outstanding engineers. It is autonomous in its administration and in the selection of its members, sharing with the National Academy of Sciences the responsibility for advising the federal government. The National Academy of Engineering also sponsors engineering programs aimed at meeting national needs, encourages education and research, and recognizes the superior achievements of engineers. Dr. Robert M. White is president of the National Academy of Engineering.

The Institute of Medicine was established in 1970 by the National Academy of Sciences to secure the services of eminent members of appropriate professions in the examination of policy matters pertaining to the health of the public. The Institute acts under the respnsibility given to the National Academy of Sciences by its congressional charter to be an adviser to the federal government and, upon its own initiative, to identify issues of medical care, research, and education. Dr. Samuel O. Thier is president of the Institute of Medicine.

The National Research Council was organized by the National Academy of Sciences in 1916 to associate the broad community of science and technology with the Academy's purposes of furthering knowledge and advising the federal government. Functioning in accordance with general policies determined by the Academy, the Council has become the principal operating agency of both the National Academy of Sciences and the National Academy of Engineering in providing services to the government, the public, and the scientific and engineering communities. The Council is administered jointly by both Academies and the Institute of Medicine. Dr. Frank Press and Dr. Robert White are chairman and vice chairman, respectively, of the National Research Council.

This work relates to the Department of the Navy Grant N00014-85-6-0093 issued by the Office of Naval Research and Department of the Army Grants MDA903-88-C-0031 and MDA903-89-K-0074 issued by the Defense Supply Service Washington. However, the content does not necessarily reflect the position or the policy of the Government, and no official endorsement should be inferred.

Library of Congress Catalog Card No. 89-64440
International Standard Book Number 0-309-04199-6

Additional copies of this report are available from:

National Academy Press
2101 Constitution Avenue N.W.
Washington, D.C. 20418
S103

Printed in the United States of America

First Printing, April 1990
Second Printing, July 1991

Dedicated to the memory of

Clyde H. Coombs: scholar, citizen, friend

COMMITTEE ON HUMAN FACTORS

DOUGLAS H. HARRIS (Chair), Anacapa Sciences, Inc., Santa Barbara, California
PAUL A. ATTEWELL, Department of Sociology, State University of New York, Stony Brook
MOHAMED M. AYOUB, Institute of Biotechnology, Texas Tech University
JEROME I. ELKIND, Xerox Corporation, Sunnyvale, California
MIRIAN M. GRADDICK, AT&T Corporation, Basking Ridge, New Jersey
OSCAR GRUSKY, Department of Sociology, University of California, Los Angeles
JULIAN HOCHBERG, Department of Psychology, Columbia University
THOMAS K. LANDAUER, Bell Communications Research, Morristown, New Jersey
NEVILLE P. MORAY, Department of Mechancial and Industrial Engineering, University of Illinois
RAYMOND S. NICKERSON, BBN Laboratories, Cambridge, Massachusetts
CHRISTOPHER D. WICKENS, Aviation Research Laboratory, University of Illinois
ROBERT C. WILLIGES, Department of Industrial Engineering and Operations Research, Virginia Polytechnic Institute and State University
J. FRANK YATES, Department of Psychology, University of Michigan

HAROLD P. VAN COTT, Study Director
BEVERLY M. HUEY, Research Associate
ELIZABETH F. NEILSEN, Research Associate
SARA K. WAMSLEY, Senior Secretary

PARTICIPANTS
WORKSHOP ON DISTRIBUTED DECISION MAKING

Baruch Fischhoff (Cochair), Department of Social & Decision Sciences, Department of Engineering & Public Policy, Carnegie Mellon University, Pittsburgh, Pennsylvania

Oscar Grusky (Cochair), Department of Sociology, University of California, Los Angeles

Kathleen Carley, Department of Social & Decision Sciences, Carnegie Mellon University, Pittsburgh, Pennsylvania

Clyde Coombs, Department of Psychology, University of Michigan

Robyn Dawes, Department of Social & Decision Sciences, Carnegie Mellon University, Pittsburgh, Pennsylvania

Stanley Deutsch, Study Director (1985–1987), Committee on Human Factors

Ralph Disney, Department of Industrial Engineering, Texas A & M University, Houston, Texas

Larry Hirschhorn, Wharton Center for Applied Research, University of Pennsylvania

Milton Katz, Army Research Institute for the Behavioral and Social Sciences, Alexandria, Virginia

Gary Klein, Klein Associates, Inc., Yellow Springs, Ohio

Todd LaPorte, Institute for Governmental Studies, University of California, Berkeley

Arie Lewin, Duke University, Durham, North Carolina & National Science Foundation, Washington, D.C.

Elizabeth Pate-Cornell, Department of Industrial Engineering, Stanford University

Olle Svenson, Department of Psychology, University of Stockholm

Frederick Thompson, Center for Naval Analysis, Alexandria, Virginia

Oliver Williamson, Department of Economics, University of California, Berkeley

Foreword

The Committee on Human Factors was established in October 1980 by the Commission on Behavioral and Social Sciences and Education of the National Research Council. The committee is sponsored by the Air Force Armstrong Aeromedical Research Laboratory, the Air Force Office of Scientific Research, the Army Advanced Systems Research Office, the Army Human Engineering Laboratory, the Army Research Institute for the Behavioral and Social Sciences, the Federal Aviation Administration, the National Aeronautics and Space Administration, the National Science Foundation, the Nuclear Regulatory Commission, and the Office of Naval Research. The principal objectives of the committee are to provide new perspectives on theoretical and methodological issues, to identify basic research needed to expand and strengthen the scientific basis of human factors, and to attract scientists both within and outside the field for interactive communication and to perform needed research. The committee aims to provide a solid foundation of research as a base on which effective human factors practices can build.

Human factors issues arise in every domain in which humans interact with the products of a technological society. In order to perform its role effectively, the committee draws on experts from a wide range of scientific and engineering disciplines. Members of the committee include specialists in such fields as psychology, engineering, biomechanics, physiology, medicine, cognitive sciences, machine intelligence, computer sciences, sociology, education, and human factors engineering. Other disciplines are represented in the working groups, workshops, and symposia organized by the committee. Each of these disciplines contributes to the basic data, theory, and methods required to improve the scientific basis of human factors.

Contents

Preface

Since its inception in 1980, the Committee on Human Factors of the National Research Council has issued a series of reports regarding the state of knowledge and research needs in different areas. Some of these topics have been pursued on the committee's own initiative, whereas others were suggested by its sponsors. In 1984, two sponsors of the committee, the Office of Naval Research and the Army Research Institute for the Behavioral and Social Sciences, approached the committee to express interest in the topic of distributed decision making. After deliberation, the committee developed a workable definition of that concept in the form of a description of the task faced by "organizations in which the information and responsibility for decision making is distributed among individuals within the organization, who are often distributed geographically." The committee concluded that, although the term was new, the problem is an old one, given important new wrinkles by advances in modern technology. The committee then decided to plan and hold a workshop on this topic. The workshop was held December 3–5, 1986, in Washington, D.C.

In the course of preparing its approach to the workshop, the committee benefited greatly from briefings by John Dockery, Office of the Joint Chiefs of Staff, and staff members at the Applied Physics Laboratory of Johns Hopkins University, coordinated by Bruce Hamill. Karen Cook of the University of Washington, Zvi Lanir of Tel Aviv University, Chuck Mills of the U.S. Forest Service, Irving Mirman of Decision Process Systems, and Franklin Moses of the Army Research Institute also provided useful input. In constituting the workshop, particular attention was paid to ensuring that all disciplines relevant to the problem would be represented and that existing scientific knowledge would be brought to bear on the problem. We were fortunate to have the active participation of many distinguished individuals before, during, and after the workshop. We gratefully acknowledge the contributions of everyone who has helped us in this endeavor.

Prior to the workshop, all participants received a copy of an article by Baruch Fischhoff and Steven Johnson, "The Possibility of Distributed Decision Making." Since the human factors community had paid little attention to this area as a significant social and scientific problem, this paper provided needed background and served as a point of departure for the thinking of the workshop participants. Because of its central role, and because it provides an introduction to some of the issues and literatures of distributed decision making, the article appears as Appendix A to this report.

Three reports by participants on their own research with existing distributed decision-making systems were also valuable: one by Todd R. LaPorte on managing air traffic control, electricity utility grids, and aircraft carrier operations; another by Gary Klein on fire fighting in both urban and rural environments; and a third by Frederick Thompson on the Composite Warfare Commander approach to management of war at sea. In addition, the Report of the Presidential Commission on the Space Shuttle Challenger Accident provided workshop participants with a valuable perspective. These discussions of concrete cases provided a common pool of examples for all participants, as well as the opportunity to become familiar with one another (and one another's disciplines) by working through a problem together.

The topics discussed in the workshop and summary here are but a subset of issues comprising the domain of distributed decision making. They were chosen because the committee judged them to be of particular interest to the human factors community. Other topics, important as they may be, were excluded from the two-day format adopted.

The organizing committee for the workshop included Clyde H. Coombs, Oscar Grusky, and Baruch Fischhoff. Shortly after the workshop, Clyde died. With him, we all lost a great friend and the scientific community lost a major contributor. In a small measure of our appreciation, we dedicate this report to him. He played a significant role in its creation.

Appreciation is extended to Harold Van Cott, committee study director, who offered technical and editorial suggestions to improve the report; Elizabeth Neilsen, research associate, who coordinated workshop and publication logistics and contributed to the editing of the report; Christine McShane, CBASSE reports editor, who improved the clarity and style of the final draft; and Sara Wamsley and Carole Foote, who provided administrative and secretarial support.

Douglas H. Harris, Chair
Committee on Human Factors

Distributed Decision Making: Report of a Workshop

INTRODUCTION

The distribution of information, authority, personnel, and resources is part of the reality facing military units, companies with dispersed sales forces, forest fire fighters, diplomatic services, and negotiating teams. In addition to daunting logistics and other technical problems, these organizations face fundamental difficulties in making and coordinating decisions that will serve the interests of both the organization as a whole and the individuals within it. Part of this problem is the tension between the need to control the individuals involved and the need to let them respond to the demands of their own immediate situations; part is the difficulty of translating overall objectives into terms that will be meaningful in the diverse concrete situations encountered throughout the organization; and part is the challenge of creating incentive systems that will properly motivate personnel.

Recent changes in technology have considerably complicated these tasks. Some of these changes have been exogenous, such as increases in the complexity of an organization's environment and the speed of response demanded by it. Neither a fleet threatened by high-speed missiles, nor a multinational corporation facing round-the-clock financial trading has the opportunities for internal consultation and coordination that it might have had in a slower age. Some of these changes are endogenous, reflecting new capabilities for transmitting information to local units and monitoring their behavior. These pressures and possibilities come from developments such as teleconferencing, electronic mail, satellite communications, shared databases, and the online monitoring of employees at video display terminals. The hope of human factors research is to anticipate and understand these changes, in order to shape the design of both the technologies and the organizations that must accommodate them.

Human factors research looks at design and performance issues involving the interface between people and machines. Examples include creating effective workstations, developing communications protocols, selecting and training operators, designing displays to reveal the current status of an industrial facility, and evaluating the human side of system performance. The Committee on Human Factors has produced reports on topics as diverse as aircraft simulators, simulator sickness, multicolor displays, mental models, the safety of nuclear power plants, and computer-aided design of helicopter pilot workstations. Each problem requires the skills of somewhat different mixes of the professions contributing to human factors, which include psychology, industrial engineering, physical anthropology, applied mathematics, training, and sociology. Each requires collaboration with other specialists knowledgeable about the environment in which people perform their tasks.

Distributed decision-making systems require the full range of this expertise. Taking military command and control as an example, there is the need to design system components as diverse as communications protocols, symbolic computer displays, filing (and retrieval) schemes for contingency plans, minimally disruptive maintenance schedules, procedures for updating key personnel, specifications for when it is permissible to override computerized controls, and rules for rewarding (or disciplining) personnel. Although the particulars will be very different, roughly the same tasks can be found in setting up an air traffic control system, an integrated forest fire fighting system, a 911 telephone emergency system, an international commodities trading system, or a carrier-based naval task force.

The differences among these systems clearly call for particularized substantive expertise; however, the similarity of their functions and challenges creates the opportunity to study distributed decision-making systems as a general phenomenon. These commonalities come in part from the demands posed by life in organizations (e.g., coordination, discipline, allocation of resources), and in part from the environment created by the technologies shared by many such systems.

Although experts in certain disciplines may take the leading role in various aspects of system design, it is characteristic of these systems that they require information from a range of disciplines. For example, although operations researchers might be able to calculate the capacity of communications channels given particular communications protocols (e.g., specifying message length and frequency), their predictions will be inaccurate unless they have some estimate of how frequently users will ask to have messages repeated or decide that there is nothing really worth reporting.

Task analysts can determine the most efficient procedures for accomplishing various maintenance functions, but they may miss the effect of shift work on operators' abilities to accomplish their tasks and detect mistakes that they have made. Planners can specify what operators should do in all imaginable contingencies; however, unless they recognize the cognitive difficulties of matching concrete situations to abstract plans (especially under conditions of stress), these planners may create an illusion of predictability for those managing a system while denying needed freedom of action for those actually doing the work.

In each of these ways, system analysts need to understand how people will fill the interstices in a system's formal design. Conversely, in order to make themselves most useful, specialists in informal behavior need help in understanding the aggregate impact of various behaviors. For example, they may advocate an open line (or party line) communication system, wherein everyone has access to every message as a way to ensure that distributed decision makers have a shared mental model of the system's overall status. In addition to worrying about the psychological impact of that policy on what information operators will choose to share (knowing that everyone is listening), they also need to anticipate the communication system's ability to sustain the load it generates.

In order to meet these challenges, efforts are needed on four different levels:

1. developing better theories of distributed decision making;
2. studying empirically issues pertinent to distributed decision making;
3. generating the research methods needed for studying distributed decision making; and
4. creating the research and development community needed to address distributed decision making and ensure the transfer of research results to practice.

Possible directions for each of these tasks are discussed in the sections that follow. The discussion leads to the proposal of research topics drawn from the workshop's deliberations. What are proposed, by and large, are steps for synthesizing a coherent field of inquiry rather than next best steps for advancing existing disciplines.

THEORIES FOR DISTRIBUTED DECISION MAKING

Here, as elsewhere, it is natural to desire an encompassing theory of the phenomenon under consideration. Given the diversity of distributed decision-making systems and the variety of activities going on in each, however, this may be a misleading objective. No single theory is likely to cover all aspects of all situations. Proposing a single theory, or even a flagship theory, risks creating an illusion of understanding and suppressing concerns that do not readily find expression within that theory. An analogy might be the neglect of higher-order cognitive processes in probabilistic risk analyses of operator performance in nuclear power plants (a technique that is much better suited for modeling more mechanistic actions of people and machines)(Reason, in press). Moreover, even with an encompassing theory as an ultimate goal, it might best be reached through a series of converging, piecemeal efforts. Several directions for such efforts are described here.

Exploring Alternative Definitions

Decision-making responsibility is distributed in almost any human enterprise. Whether it is a Neolithic hunting party or a couple working out of a common checking account or raising children together, people must coordinate their actions. Their techniques for doing so include sharing information, jointly creating contingency plans, and directly communicating instructions. (Some theorists would argue that individuals contain within themselves multiple actors whose actions must be integrated.)

Distributed decision making is a neologism that has been deliberately chosen to capture the cumulative change in the nature of multiperson decision making that has been wrought through advances in technology. Those advances have increased the distance over which individuals can maintain contact, the speed with which information and instructions can be shared, the amount of information being created and the accompanying informational load, the opportunities for monitoring operators' behavior, and the possibilities for automating instructions (e.g., through expert systems, computerized pattern recognition).

There does not, however, seem to be agreement on exactly what the new term means. This could be viewed as a barrier to effective and coordinated research. However, it could also constitute an opportunity for theoretical research, clarifying the meaning and implications of alternative definitions. That research could consider what can be distributed in distributed decision-making systems (e.g., information used in planning decisions, responsibility for making choices, accountability for those choices, the direct impact of actions, opportunities to receive feedback, the ability to change course or override plans). It could also consider over what these things are being distributed (e.g., time, space, individuals, units), the sequencing of the distribution (e.g., sequential, simultaneous), the nature of the distributional network (e.g., hierarchical, horizontal), and the relevance of external factors (e.g., time pressure, interruption of network, noise in transmission, uncertainty of outcomes). These dimensions of distributed decision making could be considered in isolation and in combination. There decision making could be considered in isolation and in combination. There seems to be great opportunity for creative thinking about these dimensions and considerable reason to resist preemptively deciding that a particular kind of system captures the essence of distributed decision making.

Improving the Availability of Existing Theories

The choice of dimensions to incorporate in alternative definitions of distributed decision making requires some expectations regarding their importance for organizational functioning. The natural source of such expectations (other than raw intuition) is existing theories regarding various components of distributed decision-making systems. Thus, theories of perception might suggest factors of systems that affect people's sensitivity to changes in their environment; theories of higher-order cognition might suggest the factors influencing the interpretation of those changes; and economic theories might suggest how operators will convert those interpretations into actions, as they try to act both in their own best interests and as agents of the overall organization.

No individual or discipline can pretend to have detailed understanding of more than a few of these perspectives. In order to avoid lopsided approaches to the problem, an encompassing perspective is needed. Without it one risks, as suggested earlier, elegant mathematical models of systems operation based on overly simple assumptions about human behavior, as well as designs based on behavioral principles that are sensible locally but have unimagined side effects when embedded in a complete operating system.

A minimal approach to breaching these barriers is making the different relevant theories generally accessible. Some progress here might be made simply through the sharing of focal papers in each discipline, perhaps accompanied by some exercises for testing comprehension. In practice, though, any discipline is likely to find other disciplines' in-house publications moderately tough going, yielding insight into those disciplines' (unstated) fundamental assumptions only with difficulty. A more attractive enterprise would be a set of commissioned chapters, each explicating the basic perspective and key results of one discipline as they apply to distributed decision making. These might be built on existing handbook chapters created for even more general audiences. The set of volumes being produced by the National Research Council's Committee on Contributions of Behavioral and Social Science to the Prevention of Nuclear War (Tetlock et al., 1989, 1990) might be a prototype of such an effort.

Extending the Range of Existing Theories

The review process for a set of chapters like that just suggested would have to ensure fidelity to the home discipline, clarity of presentation, and applicability to distributed decision making. Achieving that last goal to any reasonable extent may be a tall order for an expository chapter. As a result, there would also be a place for theoretical analyses exploring the extension of existing theoretical approaches to this new domain.

An article by Fischhoff and Johnson (Appendix A) that was circulated to participants prior to the workshop adopted one approach to that goal. It begins by describing briefly the general research paradigm, assumptions, and results of behavioral decision theory (which studies intuitive processes of judgment and decision making with something of an emphasis on when they produce suboptimal performance of the sort that might be ameliorated by training or decision aids). It then goes on to consider how those behavioral patterns might be affected by various features of distributed decision-making systems (e.g., the number of people involved, the heterogeneity of their functions, the interruptibility of their communications). Finally, it speculatively extracts possible design implications. (For example: The successful functioning of most organizations depends heavily on their operators' detailed knowledge of the imperfections in their performance. Any change in the system threatens that "local knowledge." As a result, a deliberate change in the system could only be justified if it made enough of a positive difference to outweigh the necessary loss in operators' understanding of the system's quirks. Thus, technological improvements had better be very good if they are not to reduce performance.)

In articles submitted to the workshop, Marie-Elizabeth Pate-Cornell (1984, 1986) showed how the methods of probabilistic risk analysis could be used to illuminate certain aspects of system function, such as the relationship between reliability and thresholds for action. It could naturally be extended to the effect of reporting structures and protocols on the quality of information transmission and the resulting pattern of errors in performance. An article submitted by Oliver Williamson (1981) suggested the roles of transaction costs and incentive structures on the nature and efficacy of the decisions made within an organization. This perspective might be extended to considering the result of combining subunits having internally coherent, but externally inconsistent incentive structures. Articles submitted by Ralph Disney and Dieter Konig (1985; see also Clarke and Disney, 1985) showed the richness of the models potentially available for characterizing the queuing of messages and actions in a complex organization. These alternatives could be profitably analyzed in terms of their applicability to different types of distributed decision-making systems. Each of the other articles submitted to the workshop (listed in Appendix

B) offers similiar possibilities requiring detailed interdisciplinary research. In these extensions it seems essential to stretch existing theories to cover as much of the problem as possible, rather than leaving them with those pieces of the puzzle with which they are most comfortable.

EMPIRICAL RESEARCH FOR DISTRIBUTED DECISION MAKING

Applying existing theories to distributed decision-making systems requires some perception of which features of their design are most important to their operation. To some extent, that perception may come from existing research or direct experience with particular systems. However, to a large extent, it represents disciplined speculation, extrapolating from existing theory or data. Clearly, there are many questions bearing direct empirical study in order to guide theory development and provide direct input to designers. As a first approximation, these topics can be divided into those concerning the behavior of individuals acting alone, those concerning the interaction of individuals with machines, those concerning the interactions of multiple individuals, and those concerning organizational behavior–all within distributed decision-making systems (although advances here would often be of interest elsewhere). A sampling of such topics follows, drawn from the discussions at the workshop. All have implications for human factors specialists, helping them either to propose designs or to anticipate the performance of designs proposed by others.

Research Topics in Individual Behavior

Mental Models

A distinctive feature of distributed decision-making systems is the interdependence of many parts, each of whose status may be constantly changing. Operators within the system must be mindful of the possibility of changes as they decide what actions to take, what information to solicit, and what information to share. Routine reporting requirements are designed to help people keep up to date; however, they may not be appropriate for all circumstances and may create a greater stream of information than can be incorporated in operators' mental picture of the system's status. Standard operating procedures are designed to direct actions in uncertain situations; however, that very uncertainty often leaves some latitude for determining exactly what situation exists at any moment.

It would be very helpful to know how (and how well) people create, maintain, and manipulate their mental pictures of such complex, dynamic systems. A point of departure for such research might be studies of people's mental models of formally defined physical systems (e.g., Chi,

Glaser and Farr, 1988; Gentner and Stevens, 1983; Johnson-Laird, 1985). The uncertainty, dynamism, and lack of closure of distributed decision-making systems would add some interesting wrinkles to that research.

Semi-analytic Cognition

The very complexity of such systems forces some serious thinking regarding the nature of decision making within them. Normative theories of decision making specify a laborious set of procedures, including listing of all relevant alternative courses of action, identifying the consequences potentially associated with each action, assessing the likelihood of each consequence, determining the relative importance (or attractiveness) of the different consequences, and combining all these considerations according to a defensible decision rule (von Winterfeldt and Edwards, 1986; Watson and Buede, 1988). Basic research into cognitive processes suggests that these are difficult mental operations under any circumstances; specific research into intuitive decision-making processes shows a variety of potential deficiencies; the speeded conditions of decision making in distributed systems should severely stress whatever capabilities people bring to it.

When questioned, the operators of complex systems often report a process more like pattern matching than decision making (Klein, 1986; Klein, Calderwood and Clinton-Cirocco, 1986). That is, they figure out what is happening in some holistic sense, then take the appropriate action. Their reports include some elements of analytic decision making (e.g., they talk about alternatives and weigh consequences), however, it seems to be much less than the full-blown treatment required by decision theory. Additional descriptive studies are clearly needed, in order to elaborate on these accounts and clarify how well actual behavior corresponds to this recounting. Such studies could be accompanied by theoretical treatment of the optimality (or suboptimality) of decision making by pattern matching. If there is a case to be made for pattern matching, then one could examine how it could be facilitated through the provision and display of information (and perhaps what changes in analytic decision aids might make them seem more useful). Conversely, system designers, in general, would want to know when pattern matching leads one astray. In defense systems, designers would want to know where it creates vulnerability to being led astray. Relevant literatures include those regarding the validity of introspections (e.g., Ericsson and Simon, 1980; Goldberg, 1968; Nisbett and Wilson, 1977) and the diagnostic ability of experts (e.g., Chase and Simon, 1973; Chi et al., 1988; Elstein, Shulman, and Sprafka, 1978; Goldberg, 1968; Henrion and Fischhoff, 1986).

Decision Making in Real Life

As mentioned briefly in the preceding section, an extensive literature has developed documenting deficiencies in intuitive judgment and decision-making processes (e.g., Dawes, 1979, 1988; Fischhoff, 1988; Hogarth, 1988; Kahneman, Slovic, and Tversky, 1982). Although enough studies have been done with experts performing tasks in their fields of expertise to establish that these results are not just laboratory curiosities, the vast majority of studies have still come from artificial tasks using lay subjects. As a result, there is the natural concern about their generalizability and even about whether apparently suboptimal behavior actually serves some higher goal (e.g., reflecting the occasional errors produced by generally valid judgmental strategies, reflecting strategies that pay off over a longer run than that inferred by the investigator) (Berkeley and Humphreys, 1982; Hogarth, 1988).

When human performance is suboptimal, there is the need for training, decision aids, or planning for problems. In addition to providing additional impetus for addressing these topics of general interest, distributed decision-making systems create a variety of new circumstances that may exacerbate or ameliorate the problems. Appendix A to this report speculates on some of these possibilities, which were discussed at some length during the workshop.

Interpreting Instructions

The pattern-matching process described above seems to involve interpreting concrete real-life situations in terms of some fundamental categories that people (experts) have created through experience. A complementary task, which may have quite a different cognitive dynamic, is interpreting real-life experiences in terms of general instructions provided by those higher up in an organization. These might be contingency plans, of the form "If X happens, do Y," or rules specifying goals at a fairly high level of abstraction (e.g., "Act as though Quality is Job One"). A cognitive challenge in the former case is achieving enough fluency with the abstract categories to be able to identify them with actual contingencies in the way intended by the contingency planners. If operators are unsuccessful, then decision-making authority has not been distributed in the way intended. A cognitive challenge in the latter case is to adapt hard abstract rules to murky situations (e.g., "Should I really shut down the assembly line because the paint looks a little spotty?"). If operators are unsuccessful, then system designers have failed to create the incentive schemes that they thought they had. Points of departure for these topics include studies of categorization processes for natural and artificial categories (e.g., Murphy and Medin, 1985), interpretations of reward structures (e.g., Roth, 1987), and lay theories of system behavior (e.g., Furnham, 1988).

Research Topics in Individual-Machine Behavior

Trust

Distributed decision-making systems often execute their actions through machines (e.g., missiles, reactor control rods, automatic pilots). They always coordinate those actions through machines (e.g., telecommunications networks, automated monitoring systems, data exchanges). The human operators of the system always must ask themselves whether the machines can be trusted. Will they do what I tell them to? Are they telling me the truth about how things are? Have they transmitted the messages as they were sent? Obvious (and different) kinds of errors can arise from trusting too much and trusting too little. The designers of a system want it not only to be reliable, but also to seem as reliable as it is. In some cases, they might even want to sacrifice a little actual reliability for more realistic operator expectations (Fischhoff and MacGregor, 1986).

Expectations for the components of distributed decision-making systems presumably draw on cognitive processes akin to those used in predicting the behavior of humans and machines in other situations (e.g., Fischhoff, MacGregor, and Blackshaw, 1987; Furnham, 1988; Moray, 1987a, 1987b; Moray and Rotenberg, 1989; Murphy and Winkler, 1984; Reason, in press). An obvious research strategy is to examine the generalizability of these results. A second strategy is to study the impact of features unique to distributed decision-making systems. One such feature shared by some undistributed systems is what has been called the supervisory control problem (National Research Council, 1985), the need for operators to decide when an automated system has gone sufficiently astray for them to override it (Muir, 1988). In doing so, they may be expressing mistrust, not only of the system's choice of actions, but also of its reading of the real world (e.g., based on the reports of sensors and their interpretation) and its theory of how to respond to that reality. A third strategy is to record the operation of actual systems, eliciting operators' confidence in them in ways that can be subsequently calibrated against actual performance. A fourth strategy is to look at operators' interpretations of the claims made for new equipment before it is introduced and how those expectations change (for better or worse) with experience.

Expert Systems

One variant on this general theme of trust and trustworthiness, discussed at some length at the workshop, concerned expert systems, that is, computerized systems intended to incorporate the wisdom of the most accomplished experts regarding a particular category of problem. These systems could be allowed to operate on their own unless overriden by operators (e.g., systems for deciding whether incoming missles are hostile) or could be queried as to how the expert in the machine would respond to the current situation, in terms of the way it has been described to it. There is a strong technological imperative pushing the development of expert systems for an ever-increasing range of situations. This imperative should be particularly strong in distributed decision-making systems because the promise of having a proxy expert online in the machines available at remote sites seems like an obvious way of maintaining a consistent policy and centralized control throughout.

Like any other decision aid, the contribution of expert systems to system performance depends both on their capabilities and on the appropriateness of the faith placed in those capabilities. In this light, any improvements in expert systems should improve their usefulness for distributed decision-making systems, provided that their limitations are equally well understood. Specifically, operators must understand what expert systems do and how well they do it. They must know, for example, what values a system incorporates and how well those correspond to the values appropriate to their situation (e.g., "Was the expert of the system more or less cautious in reaching decisions than I want to be?"). They must also know how their world differs from that in which the expert operated (e.g., "Did the expert have more trustworthy reporting systems? Did the expert have to consider deliberate deception when interpreting reports?"). They must know if they have advantages denied to the expert (e.g., the ability to draw on additional kinds of expertise beyond that lodged in even the most knowledgeable single individual in the world).

In addition to the cognitive challenge of improving the interpretability of expert systems for individual operators, there is also the institutional challenge of managing the allocation of responsibility for decisions made by expert systems (or by the operators who override them). This need creates a special case of the general problem of understanding institutional incentive structures.

System Stability and Operator Competence

No system in a complex, dynamic environment works exactly as planned. That is why there are still human operators, even in cases in which actions are executed by machine. The role of these operators must therefore come from knowing things that are unknown to the machine, perhaps because its formalized language cannot accommodate them, perhaps because there is inadequate theoretical understanding of the domain in which the system operates, perhaps because the theory has known flaws. In any case, the operators must have some local knowledge or indigenous technical knowledge or tacit knowledge allowing them to pick up where the machine leaves off (Brokensha, Warren, and Werner, 1980; Chi et al., 1988; Foucault, 1980; Moray, 1987b; Polanyi, 1962; Rasmussen, 1983, 1986).

Knowing more about the quality of this unique human knowledge would obviously help in guiding the allocation of responsibility between person and machine. Knowing more about the nature of this knowledge would help to understand the impact of changes in a distributed decision-making system on its operability—and about procedures for maintaining (or restoring) this kind of expertise. For example, is it better to examine potentially significant changes constantly to determine their effect on one's understanding? Or is it better to conduct periodic reviews, looking for aggregate impacts that might be more readily discernible—recognizing that one may be functioning with an outdated model between reviews?

Finally, such knowledge should help manage those changes that are controllable. There may be little that one can do to retard an opponent's adoption of a new weapons system (with its somewhat unpredictable impact on the operation of one's own systems) or on the spread of an illicit drug or unfamiliar virus in the population (with their effect on the interpretation of lab results). However, one may have some control over the introduction of new technologies that can reduce operators' understanding of their own system—either by disrupting the operational patterns that they know well or by reducing their direct contact with the system (a sort of intellectual deskilling). Given the imperatives of innovation, it would take quite solid documentation of operators' world views to resist changes in technology on the grounds that it will reduce their understanding.

Displaying Uncertainty

If systems are known to be imperfect, it is incumbent on their designers to convey that information. A fairly bounded design problem that came up several times during the workshop was how to display information about the uncertainty in a system. This general category includes several different kinds of uncertainty: that surrounding direct measurements (e.g., the temperature in a reactor core, the altitude of an aircraft), that surrounding interpreted data (e.g., the identity of an aircraft, its likely flight path), and that surrounding its recommendations (e.g., whether to shoot). Such displays would be attempts to create realistic expectations. Whether such good intentions achieve the intended effects is a potentially difficult design question, especially when the uncertainty arises from imperfect theories (even when those are applied to integrating perfect observations).

Research Topics in Multiple Individual Behavior

Shared Knowledge

The individuals (or units) in a distributed decision-making system are meant to have a shared concept of their mission (i.e., objectives and situation) at a fairly high level of generality that nonetheless allows them to function effectively in the restricted environment for which they have more detailed knowledge. Achieving this goal is in part a matter of training, so that distributed operators share certain common conceptions, and in part a matter of distributing current information, so that they stay in touch conceptually. Insofar as it is impossible to tell everybody everything, the designers of a system need to know what is the minimal level of explicit sharing needed to ensure adequate convergence of views. They also need to know what kind of information is most effectively shared (e.g., raw observations or interpretations). Conversely, they need to know the drift in perceptions that arises from lack of sharing, whether due to individuals having too much to say, having too much to listen to, or being denied the opportunity to communicate. Such knowledge would guide them in determining the capacity needed for communication channels, the fidelity needed for those channels, and the protocols for using them (e.g., when to speak, how to interpret silence). Approaches to these questions range from observational studies of the conversational norms of intact communities to mathematical models of the impact of sharing on the creation of communities (Carley, 1986a, 1986b, 1988; Grice, 1975; Hilton, 1988)

Barriers to Sharing

Communication involves more than just the transmission of propositional statements. People read between the lines of other people's statements. People read the vocal intonations and facial expressions accompanying statements for additional cues as to what is intended and what to believe. These are well-worked topics in social psychology, whose implications for distributed decision-making systems need to be understood (e.g., Spencer and Ekman, 1986; Fiske and Taylor, 1984).

In addition, there are special features of such systems that threaten to disrupt normal patterns of communication, interpretation, and understanding. For example, modern telecommunications may deprive users of necessary interpretative cues, a fact that may or may not be apparent to both transmitters and receivers of messages. They may disrupt the timing (or sequencing) messages and responses, delaying feedback and reducing coordination. Restricted communications can also prevent the unintended communication of peripheral information. Consider, for example, people who come off poorly on television not because they are uncertain of their messages, but because of discomfort with the medium. Or consider whether there would be better communication between U.S. and Soviet leaders were the current hot line replaced by a higher-fidelity channel, thereby letting through more cultural cues that might be subject to misinterpretation. These questions are beginning to receive systematic attention through both controlled experiments and detailed observational studies (e.g., Hiltz, 1984; Kiesler, Siegel, and McGuire, 1984; Meshkati, in press; Sproull and Kiesler, 1986). More research is needed, directed toward the particular conditions created by distributed decision-making systems.

Distribution of Responsibility

Organizations of any sort must allocate responsibility for their various functions. For distributed decision-making systems, this allocation must, by definition, include the collection, sharing, and interpretation of information, as well as the decision to undertake various classes of actions. These are obvious parts of its design, which would exist even were there no technology involved at all. Considering technology raises a few issues calling for particular input from human factors specialists. One is how the distribution of technical knowledge about the equipment affects control over the system. Particularly under time pressure, technically qualified operators may have to take actions without adequate opportunity to consult with their superiors (e.g., the flight deck chiefs on carriers who are career noncommissioned officers, yet subordinate to officers who are there because they have more generalized expertise) (LaPorte, 1984; Rochlin, in press). Even without time pressure, differences in social status may restrict communication, so that technically skilled operators are required to follow orders that do not make sense to someone on the shop floor. In either circumstance, the welfare of the system as a whole may require out-of-role behavior by its operators. Designers should want a better understanding of when such situations arise, how they can be minimized, and how to deal with their aftermath without undermining an organization's authority structure.

A rather different impact of technology on the distribution of responsibility is its effect on the opportunities for monitoring the performance of operators. Successful organizations require an appropriate balance between central control and local autonomy. Operators need some independence both for motivational and functional reasons. Motivationally, they need to feel that someone is not on their case all the time. Functionally, they must be able to exploit whatever unique advantages their local knowledge gives them, so that they can improvise solutions to problems that are not fully understood by those at the top. Much organizational theory deals with how to achieve this balance. In practice, though, these designs probably specify no more than necessary conditions for balance, within which real people might be able to negotiate workable arrangements. Any change in technology (or in the external world) could destabilize this balance. The increased capacity for surveillance may become a recurrent destabilizing factor in distributed decision-making systems. If those at the top of a system must know everything they can know, they may then receive a flood of information that is inadequate to assert effective control, but enough to restrict the ability of local operators to innovate. Where this happens, changes in the technology or its management are needed (Lanir, Fischhoff, and Johnson, 1988).

Research Topics in Organizational Behavior

Most of the research topics described in the preceding sections concern the reality facing individuals in distributed decision-making systems and how their performance may be improved by better design of equipment and procedures. A common assumption of these potential interventions is that an organization will be better if the performance of its constituents is improved. While this is doubtless true in general, certain phenomena emerge most clearly at the organizational level. Although these topics may seem somewhat distant from traditional human factors work, the workshop participants felt that they were essential for deploying human factors resources effectively and for understanding the impacts (intended and unintended) of interventions.

Reliability

Organizations can fail in many ways. Knowing the ways that are most likely can focus efforts on improving design or help one to choose among competing designs. Detailed quantitative modeling of organizational reliability might highlight such vulnerabilities (Pate-Cornell, 1984, 1986) for example, which methods of distributing information are most robust with regard to noise and interruptions? Human factors specialists could not only take direction from such analyses, but also give them shape by characterizing the probability of failures arising from various operator problems (Swain and Gutman, 1983). While the methods used for modeling mechanical systems (e.g., McCormick, 1981; U.S. Nuclear Regulatory Commission, 1983) are an obvious place to start such analyses, there is important theoretical ground to be broken by incorporating in them those forms of vulnerabilities that are unique to single or interacting individuals (e.g., shared misconceptions, refusals to cooperate, the ability to deceive and be deceived).

Conflicting Demands

Many organizations face conflicting demands. For example, they may have to act in both crisis and routine situations; they may have to maintain a public face quite at odds with their internal reality (e.g., exuding competence when all is chaos underneath); or they may need to adhere to procedures (or doctrine) while experimenting in order to develop better procedures. Each of these conflicting roles may call for different equipment, different procedures, different personnel, different patterns of authority, and different incentive schemes. Mediating these conflicts is essential to organizational survival. An understanding of these conflicts is essential if human factors specialists are to see where they fit in and to create designs that serve both purposes.

Learning

Like individuals, successful organizations are continually learning, both about their environment and about themselves. Their design can facilitate or hinder both the acquisition of such understanding and its distribution throughout the organization (both at any given time and over time). Human factors work may have leverage on learning processes through the methods by which experience is accumulated and disseminated. Because such change and maintenance are not always part of an organization's explicit mission, they may need to be studied and identified lest they be ignored.

Research Methods for Distributed Decision Making

Each of the research topics cited in the previous section of the report has particular methodological demands. Although those could be left to the individuals undertaking each task, there are also some recurrent needs that might be addressed profitably by research that is primarily methodological in character. The workshop identified a number of such topics, which are described below.

Analytical Measures

As mentioned, the label *distributed decision making* covers a very wide variety of organizations. Although each deserves attention in its own right, respecting its peculiarities, the accumulation of knowledge requires the ability to make more general statements about different kinds of distributed decision-making systems. That goal would be furthered by the development of broadly applicable analytical measures. For example:

- degree of distribution of decision-making authority
- degree of distribution of information
- heterogeneity of tasks across the system/degree of human and physical asset specialization
- stability of external environment
- heterogeneity of external environments
- variation in organizational demands (e.g., across steady-state and peak-load situations)
- stability of internal environment (e.g., personnel turnover, technological change)
- irreversibility of actions
- time stress

Case Studies

Detailed case studies of actual distributed decision-making systems are needed, both for individual disciplines to make contact between their existing theories and this complex reality, and for them to make contact with one another. Establishing a database of case studies created for these purposes would help achieve these goals. Such studies would have to provide the information needed by the different relevant disciplines and avoid preemptive interpretation of what has happened. Assembling such a canonical set might begin with existing case studies, reviewing them for the features that are missing and might be supplemented. Even if individually adequate studies are currently available, the set of existing studies would have to be reviewed for sampling biases. For example, it might unduly emphasize crisis situations (in which organizations are tested) and calamities (in which they fail the test).

Instrumentation

Case studies are usually fictions to some extent because they rely on retrospective reports. Even central participants might not remember what they themselves have done in a particular situation (e.g., because it no longer makes sense, given what they now know about what was really happening) (Dawes, 1988; Ericsson and Simon, 1980; Pew, Miller, and Feeher, 1981). Especially central participants may be reluctant to reveal what they know, in order to present themselves in a more favorable light. In addition, critical events may simply go unobserved. As a result, it would be helpful to automatically log or record ongoing systems operation for the sake of later analysis. This might involve developing black boxes to record events, online interrogation procedures to question operators about what they think is happening, observational techniques cueing investigators to potentially significant occurrences, or even the creation of experimental systems, operating long enough for participants to achieve stable behavior patterns under the watchful eyes of investigators (Moray, 1986).

Capturing Mental Models

Inevitably, the study of distributed decision-making systems must rely on operators' reports of what they think is or was happening. For the foreseeable future, that is likely to be an irreplaceable source of insight regarding the subjective reality that it creates for them. Distributed decision-making systems pose particularly difficult challenges for such elicitation. The events are complex and dynamic; participants often have an incomplete understanding of what was happening; reports require inferences, rather than mere observation; and critical events may have to be translated from visual (or even visceral) experiences to verbal statements. Improved methods are needed for eliciting what only participants can know (Gentner and Stevens, 1983; Lehner and Adelman, 1987; Moray, 1987a).

Institutional Structure for Distributed Decision Making

Although there was considerable agreement among workshop participants on the importance of studying the topics raised in this report, the question of how distributed decision making should be studied was not fully resolved. Participants agreed that significant research progress depends on the creation of a research community that allows and reinforces sustained interaction among leading scholars in the various relevant disciplines, and between these scholars and substantive experts familiar with the operation of actual systems. Consideration of distributed decision-making systems raises cutting-edge issues in many disciplines. These include both topics that are unique to such systems and topics that occur elsewhere but have yet to be addressed fully. Certainly the operators and designers of such systems would benefit from universal access to existing scientific knowledge. However, these systems really deserve the attention of creative investigators breaking new ground.

There are several obstacles to creating such conditions for university-based researchers. One is the centripetal force of academic disciplines that typically reward scholars most for intradisciplinary work. A second obstacle is the need to master the nuances of concrete systems and additonal methodological procedures, which simply demand more time than can be allotted by many individuals facing the pressures of promotion and tenure. A third is the frequent lack of respect within the academic community for applied research and its often particularist conclusions.

One response to these obstacles is to look elsewhere for researchers in settings less subject to the constraints of a university-based culture, say, to a private research and consulting organization. This is an appropriate solution when such an organization can provide the kind of enrichment that comes from interdisciplinary exchanges comparable to those of an academic environment and from the rigor that comes from peer review. Some contract research organizations meet these standards; others do not. These obstacles are not, of course, unique to research on distributed decision making; that makes them no less real for sponsors of research and the managers of related systems.

The recognition of workshop participants that obstacles do exist did not dampen their enthusiasm for working on the problems that were raised nor from considering ways in which they might work on them inside or outside academia. Just how this might be done and which research topics should be given the highest priorities were questions beyond the scope of the workshop and constitute the basis for an agenda for some future effort.

References

Berkeley, D., and P. Humphreys

1982 Structuring decision problems and the "bias heuristic." *Acta Psychologica* 50:201-252.

Brokensha, D., D.M. Warren, and O. Werner

1980 *Indigenous Knowledge Systems and Development*. Baltimore: Associated Universities Press.

Carley, K.M.

1986a An approach for relating social structure to cognitive structure. *Journal of Mathematical Sociology* 12(2):137-189.

1986b Knowledge acquisition as a social phenomenon. *Instructional Science* 13:381-438.

1988 Distributed information and organizational decision-making models. In Andrew Sage, ed., *Concise Encyclopedia of Information Processing in Systems and Organizations*. New York: Pergamon Press.

Chase, W.G., and H.A. Simon

1973 Perception in chess. *Cognitive Psychology* 4:55-81.

Chi, M.T.H., R. Glaser, and M.J. Farr, eds.

1988 *The Nature Of Expertise*. Hillsdale, N.J.: Erlbaum.

Clarke, A.B., and R.L. Disney

1985 *Probability and Random Processes: A First Course with Application*. New York: J. Wiley.

Dawes, R.M.

1979 The robust beauty of improper linear models in decision making. *American Psychologist* 34:571-582.

1988 *Rational Choice In An Uncertain World*. New York: Harcourt Brace Jovanovich.

Disney, R.L., and D. Konig

1985 Queueing networks: A survey of their random processes. *Society for Industrial and Applied Mathematics* 27(3):335-403.

Elstein, A., L.S. Shulman, and S.A. Sprafka

1978 *Medical Problem Solving*. Cambridge, Mass.: Harvard University Press.

Ericsson, A., and H. Simon

1980 Verbal reports as data. *Psychological Review* 87:215-251.

Fischhoff, B.
1988 Judgment and decision making. Pp. 153-187 in R.J. Steinberg and E.E. Smith, eds., *The Psychology of Human Thought*. New York: Cambridge University Press.

Fischhoff, B., and D. MacGregor
1986 Calibrating databases. *Journal of the Society for Information Sciences* 37(4):222-233.

Fischhoff, B., D. MacGregor, and L. Blackshaw
1987 Creating categories for databases. *International Journal of Man-Machine Systems* 27:33-63.

Fiske, S., and S. Taylor
1984 *Social Cognition*. Reading, Mass.: Addison Wesley.

Foucalt, M.
1980 Georges Canguilhem—philosopher of error. *Ideology and Consciousness* 7:51-62.

Furnham, A.
1988 *Lay Theories: Everyday Understanding of Problems in the Social Sciences.* New York: Pergamon Press.

Gentner, D., and A. Stevens
1983 *Mental Models*. Hillsdale, N.J.: Erlbaum.

Goldberg, L.R.
1968 Simple models or simple processes? *American Psychologist* 23:483-496.

Grice, J.
1975 Logic and conversation. P. Cole and J.L. Morgan, eds., *Syntax and Semantics 3: Speech Acts*. New York: Academic Press.

Henrion, M., and B. Fischhoff
1986 Assessing uncertainty in physical constants. *American Journal of Physics* 54(9):791-798.

Hilton, D. ed.
1988 *Contemporary Science and Natural Explanation: Commonsense Conceptions of Causality*. New York: New York University Press.

Hiltz, S.R.
1984 *Online Communities*. Norwood, N.J.: Ablex.

Hogarth, R.
1988 *Judgment and Choice*. New York: Wiley.

Johnson-Laird, P.
1985 *Mental Models*. New York: Cambridge University Press.

Kahneman, D., P. Slovic, and A. Tversky, eds.
1982 *Judgment Under Uncertainty: Heuristics and Biases*. New York: Cambridge University Press.

Kiesler, S., J. Siegel, and T. McGuire
1984 Social psychological aspects of computer-mediated communication. *American Psychologist* 39:1123-1134.

Klein, G.
1986 *Analogical Decision Making*. Interim Report MDA903-85-C0327, prepared for Army Research Institute for the Behavioral and Social Sciences. Klein Associates, Yellow Springs, Ohio.

Klein, G., R. Calderwood, and A. Clinton-Cirocco
1986 *Rapid Decision Making On The Fire Ground*. Proceedings of the Human Factors Society 30th Annual Meeting. Santa Monica, Calif.: Human Factors Society.

Lanir, Z., B. Fischhoff, and S. Johnson
1988 Military risk taking: C3I and the cognitive functions of boldness in war. *Journal of Strategic Studies* 11(1):96-114.
LaPorte, T.R.
1984 *Technology as Social Organization*. Working paper No. 84-1. Berkeley: University of California, Institute of Governmental Studies.
Lehner, P., and L. Adelman, eds.
1987 Biases in Knowledge Engineering. Special issue of *IEEE Transactions for Systems, Man, & Cybernetics*. New York: IEEE.
McCormick, N.
1981 *Reliability Engineering*. New York: Wiley.
Meshkati, N.
in press An integrative model for designing reliable technological organizations: The role of cultural variables. In J. Rasmussen and R. Batstone, eds., *Safety Control And Risk Management*. Washington, D.C: World Bank.
Moray, N.
1986 Modeling cognitive activities: Human limitations in relation to computer aids. In E. Hollnagel, G. Mancini and D.D. Woods, eds., *Intelligent Decision Support in Process Environments*. Berlin: Springer-Verlag.
1987a Intelligent aids, mental models and the theory of machines. *International Journal of Man-machine Studies* 27:619-629.
1987b Monitoring behavior and supervisory control. In K. Boff, L. Kaufmann, and J. Thomas, eds., *Handbook of Perception and Human Performance*. New York: Wiley.
Moray, N., and I. Rotenberg
in press Fault management in process control: Eye movements and action. *Ergonomics*.
Muir, B.M.
1988 Trust between humans and machines, and the design of decision aids. In E. Hollnagel, G. Mancini and D.D. Woods, eds., *Cognitive Engineering In Complex Dynamic Worlds*. New York: Academic Press.
Murphy, A.W., and R.W. Winkler
1984 Probability of precipitation forecasts. *Journal of the American Statistical Association* 79:391-400.
Murphy, G.L., and D.L. Medin
1985 The role of theories in conceptual coherence. *Psychological Review* 92:289-316.
National Research Council
1985 *Research and Modeling of Supervisory Control Behavior*. Committee on Human Factors. Washington, D.C.: National Academy Press.
Nisbett, R.E., and T.O. Wilson
1977 Telling more than we can know: Verbal reports on mental process. *Psychological Review* 84:231-259.
Pate-Cornell, E.-M
1984 Fault trees vs. event trees in reliability analysis. *Risk Analysis* 4(3):177-186.
1986 Warning systems in risk management. *Risk Analysis* 6(2):223-234.
Pew, R., D.C. Miller, and C.E. Feeher
1981 *Evaluation Of Proposed Control Room Improvements Through Analysis Of Critical Operator Decision*. EPRI NP-1982. Palo Alto, Calif.: Electric Power Research Institute.

Polanyi, M.
1962 *Personal Knowledge*. London: Routledge & Kegan Paul.

Rasmussen, J.
1983 Skills, rules & knowledge. *IEEE Transactions for Systems, Man and Cybernetics* SMC-13:257-266.
1986 *Information Processing and Human Machine Interaction*. New York: North Holland.

Reason, J.
in press *Human Error*. Cambridge, England: Cambridge University Press.

Rochlin, E.
in press Technology, hierarchy, and organizational self-design: U.S. Naval flight operations as a case study. In J. Rasmussen and R. Batstone, eds., *Safety Control and Risk Management*. Washington, D.C.: World Bank.

Roth, A., ed.
1987 *Experimental Studies of Economic Behavior*. New York: Cambridge University Press.

Sheridan, T.
1988 The system perspective. In E.L. Wiener and D.C. Nagel, eds., *Human Factors In Aviation*. New York: Academic Press.

Spencer, K., and P. Ekman, eds.
1986 *Handbook of Nonverbal Behavior*. New York: Cambridge University Press.

Sproull, L., and S. Kiesler
1986 Reducing social context cues in electronic mail in organizational communication. *Management Science* 32:1492-1512.

Swain, A., and H.C. Gutman
1983 *Handbook of Human Reliability Analysis With Emphasis on Nuclear Power Plants*. NUREG/CR-1278. Washington, D.C.: U.S. Nuclear Regulatory Commission.

Tetlock, P.E., J.L. Husbands, R. Jervis, P. Stern, and C. Tilly, eds.
1989 *Behavior, Society, and Nuclear War*, Vol. 1. Committee on Contributions of Behavioral and Social Science to the Prevention of Nuclear War. New York: Oxford University Press.
1990 *Behavior, Society, and Nuclear War*, Vol. 2. Committee on Contributions of Behavioral and Social Science to the Prevention of Nuclear War. New York: Oxford University Press.

U.S. Nuclear Regulatory Commission
1983 *Probabilistic Risk Analysis Procedures Guide*. NURE6/CR-2300. Washington, D.C.: U.S. Nuclear Regulatory Commission.

von Winterfeldt, D., and E. Edwards
1986 *Decision Analysis and Behavioral Research*. New York: Cambridge University Press.

Watson, S. and D.H. Buede
1988 *Decision Synthesis*. Cambridge, England: Cambridge University Press.

Williamson, O.E.
1981 The economics of organization: The transaction cost approach. *American Journal of Sociology* 87(3):548-574.

Appendix A
The Possibility of Distributed Decision Making

BARUCH FISCHHOFF AND STEPHEN JOHNSON

Modern command-and-control systems and foreign affairs operations represent special cases of a more general phenomenon: having the information and authority for decision making distributed over several individuals or groups. Distributed decision-making systems can be found in such diverse settings as voluntary organizations, multinational corporations, diplomatic corps, government agencies, and married couples managing a household. Viewing any distributed decision-making system in this broader context helps to clarify its special, and not-so-special, properties. It also shows the relevance of research and experience that have accumulated elsewhere. As an organizing device, we develop a general *task analysis* of distributed decision-making systems, detailing the performance issues that accrue with each level of complication, as one goes from the simplest situation (involving a single individual intuitively pondering a static situation with complete information) to the most complex (with heterogeneous, multiperson systems facing dynamic, uncertain, and hostile environments that threaten the communication links and actors in their system). Drawing from the experience of different systems and from research in areas such as behavioral decision theory, psychology, cognitive science, sociology, and organizational development, the analysis suggests both problems and possible solutions. It also derives some general conclusions regarding the design and management of such systems, as well as the asymptotic limits to their performance and the implications of those limits for an organization and overall design strategy.

Partial support for this research was provided by the Office of Naval Research, under Contract No. N00014-85-C-0041 to Perceptronics, Inc.,"Behavioral Aspects of Distributed Decision Making."

A SHORT HISTORY OF DECISION AIDING

It is common knowledge that decision making is often hard. One of the clearest indications of this difficulty is the proliferation of decision aids, be they consultants, analyses, or computerized support systems (Humphreys, Svenson, and Vari, 1983; Stokey and Zeckhauser, 1978; Wheeler and Janis, 1980; von Winterfeldt and Edwards, 1986; Yates, 1989). Equally clear, but perhaps more subtle evidence is the variety of devices used by people to avoid analytic decision making; these include procrastination, endless pursuit of better information, reliance on habit or tradition, and even the deferral to aids when there is no particular reason to think that they can do better (Corbin, 1980). A common symptom of this reluctance to make decisions is the attempt to convert decision making, which reduces to a gamble surrounded by uncertainty regarding what one will get and how one will like it, to problem solving, which holds out the hope of finding the one right solution (Montgomery, 1983).

Somewhat less clear is just why decision making is so hard. The diversity of coping mechanisms suggests a diversity of diagnoses. The disappointing quality of the help offered by decision aids suggests that these diagnoses are at least somewhat off target. The battlefield of decision aiding is strewn with good ideas that did not quite pan out, after raising hopes and attracting attention. Among the aids that remain, some persist on the strength of the confidence inspired by their proponents and some persist on the strength of the need for help, even if the efficacy of that help cannot be established.

In retrospect, it seems as though most of the techniques that have fallen by the wayside never really had a chance. There was seldom anything sustaining them beyond their proponents' enthusiasm and sporadic ability to give good advice in specific cases. The techniques drew on no systematic theoretical base and subjected themselves to no rigorous testing.

For the past 20 to 30 years, behavioral decision theory has attempted to develop decision aids with a somewhat better chance of survival (Edwards, 1954, 1961; Einhorn and Hogarth, 1981; Pitz and Sachs, 1984; Slovic, Fischhoff, and Lichtenstein, 1977; Rappoport and Wallsten, 1972). Its hopes are pinned on a mixture of prescriptive and descriptive research. The former asks how people should make decisions, while the latter asks how they actually do make decisions. In combination, these two research programs attempt to build from people's strengths while compensating for their weaknesses. The premise of the field is that significant decisions should seldom be entrusted entirely either to unaided intuition or to automated procedures. Finding the optimal division of labor requires an understanding of where people are and where they should be. The quest for that understanding has produced enough surprises to establish that it requires an integrated program of theoretical and empirical research. Common sense is not a good guide to knowing what makes a good decision or why it is hard to identify one.

Initially, behavioral decision theory took its marching orders from standard American economics, which assumes that people always know what they want and choose the optimal course of action for getting it. Taken literally, these strong assumptions leave a narrow role for descriptive research: finding out what it is that people want by observing their decisions and working backward to identify the objectives that were optimized. These assumptions leave no role at all for prescriptive research, because people can already fend quite well for themselves. As a result, the economic perspective is not very helpful for the erstwhile decision aider—if its assumptions are true.

However, the perceived need for decision aiding indicates that the assumptions are not true. People seem to have a lot of trouble with decision making. The first, somewhat timorous, response of researchers to this discrepancy between the ideal and the reality was to document it. It proved not hard to show that people's actual performance is suboptimal (Edwards, 1954, 1961; Einhorn and Hogarth, 1981; Pitz and Sachs, 1984; Slovic, Fischhoff, and Lichtenstein, 1977; Rappoport and Wallsten, 1972). Knowing the size of the problem, at least under certain circumstances, is helpful in a number of ways: it can show how much to worry, where to be ready for surprises, where help is most needed, and how much to invest in that help. However, size estimates are not very informative about how to make matters better.

Realizing this limitation, researchers then turned their attention from what people are not doing (making optimal decisions) to what they are doing and why it is not working. Aside from their theoretical interest, such psychological perspectives offer several points of leverage for erstwhile decision aiders. One is that they allow one to predict where the problems will be greatest by describing how people respond to different situations. A second is that they help decision aiders talk to decision makers by showing how the latter think about their tasks. A third is that they show the processes that must be changed if people are to perform more effectively. Although it would be nice to make people over as model decision makers, the reality is that they have to be moved in gradual steps from where they are now.

As behavioral decision theory grew, two of the first organizations to see its potential as the foundation for new decision-aiding methods were the Advanced Research Projects Agency and the Office of Naval Research. Their joint program in decision analysis promoted the development of methods that, first, created models of the specific problems faced by individual decision makers and, then, relied on the formal procedures of decision theory to identify the best course of action in each. These methods were descriptive in the sense of trying to capture the subjective reality faced by the decision maker and prescriptive in the sense of providing advice on what to do.

Although it might have been tempting to take the (potentially flashy) technique and run with it, the program managers required regular interactions among their contractors, including psychologists, economists, decision theorists, operations researchers, computer scientists, consulting decision analysts, and even some practicing decision makers. The hope was to keep the technique from outrunning its scientific foundations. At any point in time, decision analysts should use the best techniques available. However, their decision aid will join its predecessors if they cannot eventually answer questions such as, How do you know that people can describe their decisions problems to you? What evidence is there that this improves decision making, beyond your clients' reports that it makes them feel good? (Fischhoff, 1980).

Like other good-looking products, decision analysis has taken on a life of its own, with college courses, computer programs, and consulting firms. Its relative success and longevity may owe something to the initial attention paid to its behavioral foundations. That research probably helped both by sharpening the technique and by giving it an academic patina that enhanced its marketability. Moreover, there is still a flow of basic research looking at questions such as, Can people assess the extent of their own knowledge? Can people tell when something important is missing from the description of a decision problem? Can people describe quantitatively the relative importance of different objectives (e.g., speed versus accuracy)?[1]

The better work in the field, both basic and applied, carries strong caveats regarding the quality of the help that it is capable of providing and the degree of residual uncertainty surrounding even the most heavily aided decisions. Such warnings are essential, because it is hard for the buyer to beware. People have enough experience to evaluate quality in toothpaste and politicians. However, it is hard to evaluate advice, especially when the source is unfamiliar and the nature of the difficulty is unclear. Without a sharp conception of why decision making is hard, one is hard put to evaluate attempts to make it better.

---

[1] All three of these questions refer to essential skills for effective use of decision analysis. The empirical evidence suggests that the answer to each is,"No, not really." However, there is some chance for improving their performance by properly structuring their tasks (Fischhoff, Svenson, and Slovic, 1987; Goldberg, 1968; Kahneman, Slovic, and Tversky, 1982; Slovic, Lichtenstein, and Fischhoff, 1988).

WHY IS INDIVIDUAL DECISION MAKING SO HARD?

According to most prescriptive schemes, good decision making involves the following steps:

a. Identify all possible courses of action (including, perhaps, inaction).
b. Evaluate the attractiveness (or aversiveness) of the consequences that may arise if each course of action is adopted.
c. Assess the likelihood of each consequence actually happening (should each action be taken).
d. Integrate all these considerations, using a defensible (i.e., rational) decision rule to select the best (i.e., optimal) action.

The empirical research has shown difficulties at each of these steps as described below.

Option Generation

When they think of action options, people often neglect seemingly obvious candidates. Moreover, they seem relatively insensitive to the number or importance of the omitted alternatives (Fischhoff, Slovic, and Lichtenstein, 1978; Gettys, Pliske, Manning, and Casey, 1987; Pitz, Sachs, and Heerboth, 1980). Options that would otherwise command attention are out of mind when they are out of sight, leaving people with the impression that they have analyzed problems more thoroughly than is actually the case.

Those options that are noted are often defined quite vaguely, making it difficult to evaluate them precisely, communicate them to others, follow them if they are adopted, or tell when circumstances have changed enough to justify rethinking the decision.[2] Imprecision also makes it difficult to evaluate decisions in the light of subsequent experience, insofar as it is hard to reconstruct exactly what one was trying to do and why. That reconstruction is further complicated by hindsight bias, the tendency to exaggerate in hindsight what one knew in foresight (Fischhoff, 1975, 1982). The feeling that one knew all along what was going to happen leads one to be unduly harsh on past decisions (if it was obvious what was going to happen, then failure to select the best option must mean incompetence) and to be unduly optimistic about future decisions (by encouraging the feeling that things are generally well understood, even if they are not working out so well).

[2] For discussion of such imprecision in carefully prepared formal analyses of government actions, see Fischhoff (1984) and Fischhoff and Cox (1985).

Value Assessment

Evaluating the potential consequences might seem to be the easy part of decision making, insofar as people should know what they want and like. Although this is doubtless true for familiar and simple consequences, many interesting decisions present novel outcomes in unusual juxtapositions. For example, two potential consequences that may arise when deciding whether to dye one's graying hair are reconciling oneself to aging and increasing the risk of cancer 10 to 20 years hence. Who knows what either event is *really* like, particularly with the precision needed to make trade-offs between the two? In such cases, one must go back to some set of basic values (e.g., those concerned with pain, prestige, vanity), decide which are pertinent, and determine what role to assign them. As a result, evaluation becomes an inferential problem (Rokeach, 1973).

The evidence suggests that people have trouble making such inferences (Fischhoff, Slovic, and Lichtenstein, 1980; Eogarth, 1982; National Research Council, 1981; Tversky and Kahneman, 1981). They may fail to identify all relevant values, to recognize the conflicts among them, or to reconcile those conflicts that they do recognize. As a result, the values that they express are often highly (and unwittingly) sensitive to the exact way in which evaluation questions are posed, whether by survey researchers, decision aids, politicians, merchants, or themselves. Formally equivalent versions of the same question can evoke quite different considerations and hence lead to quite different decisions. To take just three examples, (a) the relative attractiveness of two gambles may depend on whether people are asked how attractive each is or how much they would pay to play (Grether and Plott, 1979; Slovic and Lichtenstein, 1983); (b) an insurance policy may become much less attractive when its premium is described as a sure loss (Fischhoff et al., 1980; Hershey, Kunreuther, and Schoemaker, 1982); (c) a risky venture may seem much more attractive when described in terms of the lives that will be saved by it, rather than in terms of the lives that will be lost (Kahneman and Tversky, 1979; Tversky and Kahneman, 1981).

People can view most consequences in a number of different lights. How richly they do view them depends on how sensitive the evaluation process is. Questions have to be asked in some way, and how they are asked may induce random error (by confusing people), systematic errors (by emphasizing some perspectives and neglecting others), or unduly extreme judgments (by failing to evoke underlying conflicts). People appear to be ill equipped to recognize the ways in which they are manipulated by evaluation questions, in part because the idea of uncertain values is counterintuitive, in part because the manipulations prey (perhaps unwittingly) on their own lack of insight. Even consideration of their own past decisions does not provide a stable point of reference, because people have difficulty introspecting about the factors that motivated their actions (i.e., why they did things) (Ericsson and Simon, 1980; Nisbett and Wilson, 1977). Thus, uncertainty about values can be as serious a problem as uncertainty about facts (March, 1978).

Uncertainty Assessment

Although people are typically ready to recognize uncertainty about what will happen, they are not always well prepared to deal with that uncertainty (by assessing the likelihood of future events). How people do (or do not) make judgments under conditions of uncertainty has been a major topic of research for the past 15 years (Kahneman, Slovic, and Tversky, 1982). A rough summary of its conclusions would be that people are quite good at tracking repetitive aspects of their environment, but not very good at combining those observations into inferences about what they have not seen (Edwards, 1954, 1961; Einhorn and Hogarth, 1981; Pitz and Sachs, 1984; Slovic, Fischhoff, and Lichtenstein, 1977; Rappoport and Wallsten, 1972; Kahneman, Slovic, and Tversky, 1982; Brehmer, 1980; Peterson and Beach, 1967). Thus, they might be able to tell how frequently they have seen or heard about a particular cause of death, but not how unrepresentative their experience has been—leading them to overestimate risks to which they have been overexposed (Tversky and Kahneman, 1973). They can tell what usually happens in a particular situation and recognize how a specific instance is special, yet not be able to integrate those two (uncertain) facts—most often focusing on the specific information and ignoring experience (Bar Hillel, 1980). They can tell how similar a specific instance is to a prototypical case, yet not how important similarity is for making predictions—usually relying on it too much (Bar Hillel, 1984; Kahneman and Tversky, 1972). They can tell how many times they have seen an effect follow a potential cause, yet not infer what that says about causality—often perceiving correlations when none really exists (Beyth-Marom, 1982a, 1982b; Einhorn and Hogarth, 1978; Shaklee and Mimms, 1982).

In addition to these difficulties in integrating information, people's intuitive predictions are also afflicted by a number of systematic biases in how they gather and interpret information. These include overconfidence in the extent of their own knowledge (Fischhoff, 1982; Lichtenstein, Fischhoff, and Phillips, 1982; Wallsten and Budescu, 1983), underestimation of the time needed to complete projects (Armstrong, 1985; Kidd, 1970; Tihansky, 1976), unfair dismissal of information that threatens favored beliefs (Nisbett and Ross, 1980), exaggeration of personal immunity to various threats (Svenson, 1981; Weinstein, 1980), insensitivity to the speed with which exponential processes accelerate (Wagenaar and Sagaria, 1976), and oversimplification of others' behavior (Mischel, 1968; Rose, 1977).

Option Choice

Decision theory is quite uncompromising regarding the sort of rule that people should use to integrate all of these values and probabilities in the quest of a best alternative. Unless some consequences are essential, it should be an expectation rule, whereby an option is evaluated according to the attractiveness of its consequences, weighted by their likelihood of being obtained (Schoemaker, 1983). Since it has become acceptable to question the descriptive validity of this rule, voluminous research has looked at how well it predicts behavior (Feather, 1982).

A rough summary of this work would be that: (a) it often predicts behavior quite well—if one knows how people evaluate the likelihood and attractiveness of consequences; (b) with enough ingenuity, one can usually find some set of beliefs (regarding the consequences) for which the rule would dictate choosing the option that was selected—meaning that it is hard to prove that the rule was not used; (c) expectation rules can often predict the outcome of decision-making processes even when they do not at all reflect the thought processes involved—so that predicting behavior is not sufficient for understanding or aiding it (Fischhoff, 1982).

More process-oriented methods revealed a more complicated situation. People seldom acknowledge using anything as computationally demanding as an expectation rule or feel comfortable using it when it is proposed to them (Lichtenstein, Slovic, and Zink, 1969). To the extent that they do compute, they often seem to use quite different rules (Kahneman and Tversky, 1979; Tversky and Kahneman, 1981; Beach and Mitchell, 1978; Payne, 1982). Indeed, they even seem unimpressed by the assumptions used to justify the expectation rule (Slovic and Tversky, 1974). To the extent that they do not compute, they use a variety of simple rules whose dictates may be roughly similar to those of the expectation rule or may be very different (Beach and Mitchell, 1978; Payne, 1982; Janis and Mann, 1977; Tversky, 1969). Many of these can be summarized as an attempt to avoid making hard choices by finding some way to view the decision as an easy choice (e.g., by eliminating consequences on which the seemingly best option rates poorly) (Montgomery, 1983).

Cognitive Assets and Biases

This (partial) litany of the problems described by empirical researchers paints quite a dismal picture of people's ability to make novel (or analytical) decisions, so much so that the investigators doing this work have been accused of being problem mongers (Berkeley and Humphreys, 1982; Jungermann, 1984; von Winterfeldt and Edwards, 1986). Of course, if one hopes to help people (in any arena), then the problems are what matter, for they provide a point of entry. In addition to meaning well, investigators in this area have also had a basically respectful attitude toward the objects of their studies. It is not people, but their performance, that is shown in a negative light. Indeed, in the history of the social sciences, the interest in judgmental biases came as part of a cognitive backlash to psychoanalysis, with its dark interpretation of human foibles. The cognitive perspective showed how biases could emerge from honest, unemotional thought processes.

Typically, these mini-theories show people processing information in reasonable ways that often work well but can lead to predictable trouble. A simple example would be relying on habit or tradition as a guide to decision making. That might be an efficient way of making relatively good decisions, but it would lead one astray if conditions had changed or if those past decisions reflected values that were no longer applicable. A slightly more sophisticated example is reliance on the "availability heuristic" for estimating the likelihood of events for which adequate statistical information is missing. This is a rule of thumb by which events are judged likely if it is easy to imagine them happening or remember them having occurred in the past. Although it is generally true that more likely events are more available, use of the rule might lead to exaggerating the likelihood of events that have been overreported in the media or are the topic of personal worry (Tversky and Kahneman, 1973).

Reliance on these simple rules seems to come from two sources. One is people's limited mental computation capacity; they have to simplify things in order to get on with life (Miller, 1956; Simon, 1957). The second is their lack of training in decision making, leading them to come up with rules that make sense but have not benefited from rigorous scrutiny (Beyth-Marom, Dekel, Gombo, and Shaked, 1985). Moreover, people's day-to-day experience does not provide them with the conditions (e.g., prompt, unambiguous feedback) needed to acquire judgment and decision making as learned skills. Experience does often allow people to learn the solutions to specific repeated problems through trial and error. However, things get difficult when one has to get it right the first time.

WHAT CAN BE DONE ABOUT IT?

The down side of this information-processing approach is the belief that many problems are inherent in the way that people think about making decisions. The up side is that it shows specific things that might be done to get people to think more effectively.

Just looking at the list of problems suggests some procedures that might be readily incorporated in automated (online) decision aids (as well as their low-tech human counterparts). To counter the tendency to neglect significant options or consequences, an aid could provide checklists with generic possibilities (Beach, Townes, Campbill, and Keating, 1976; Hammer, 1980; Janis, 1982). To reduce the tendency for overconfidence, an aid could force users to list reasons why they might be wrong before assessing the likelihood that they are right (Koriat, Lichtenstein, and Fischhoff, 1980). To discourage hindsight bias, an aid can preserve the decision makers' history and rationale (showing how things once looked) (Slovic and Fischhoff, 1977). To avoid incomplete value elicitation, an aid could force users to consider alternative perspectives and reconcile the differences among them. At least these seem like plausible procedures; whether they work is an empirical question. For each intervention, one can think of reasons why it might not work, at least if done crudely (e.g., long checklists might reduce the attention paid to individual options, leading to broad but superficial analysis).

Modeling Languages

One, or the, obvious advantage of computerized aids is their ability to handle large amounts of information rapidly. The price paid for rapid information handling is the need to specify a model for the computer's work. This model could be as simple as a list of key words for categorizing and retrieving information or as complex as a full-blown decision analysis (Behn and Vaupel, 1983; Brown, Kahr, and Peterson, 1974; Keeney and Raiffa, 1976; Raiffa, 1968) or risk analysis (McCormick, 1981; U.S. Nuclear Regulatory Commission, 1983; Wilson and Crouch, 1982) within which all information is incorporated. However user friendly an aid might be, using a model means achieving a degree of abstraction that is uncommon for many people. For example, even at the simplest level, it may be hard to reduce a substantive domain to a set of key words. Moreover, any model is written in something like a foreign language, with a somewhat strange syntax and vocabulary. Successful usage means being able to translate what one knows into terms that the modeling language (and the aid) can understand. Any lack of fluency on the part of the user or any restrictions on the language's ability to capture certain realities reflects a communication disorder limiting the aid's usefulness.

For example, probabilistic risk analyses provide a valuable tool for figuring out how complex technical systems, such as nuclear power or chemical plants, operate and how they will respond to modifications. They do this by representing the system by the formal connections among its parts (e.g., showing how failures in one sector will affect performance in others).

Both judgment and statistics are used to estimate the model's parameters. In this way, it is possible to pool the knowledge of many experts, expose that knowledge to external review, compute the overall performance of the system, and see how sensitive that performance is to variations (or uncertainties) in those parameters. (These are just the sort of features that one might desire in an aid designed to track and project the operation of a military command.) Yet current modeling languages require the experts to summarize their knowledge in quantitative and sometimes unfamiliar terms, and they are ill suited to represent human behavior (such as that of the system's operators) (Fischhoff, 1988). As a result, the model is not reality. Moreover, it may differ in ways that the user understands poorly, just as the speaker of a foreign language may be insensitive to its nuances. At some point, the user may lose touch with the model without realizing it. The seriousness of this threat with particular aids is an empirical question that is just beginning to receive attention (National Research Council, 1983).

Skilled Judgment

Whether or not one relies on an aid, a strong element of judgment is essential to all decision making. With unaided decision making, judgment is all. With an aid, it is the basis for creating the model, estimating its parameters, and interpreting its results. Improving the judgments needed for analysis has been the topic of intensive research, with moderately consistent (although incomplete) results, some of them perhaps surprising (Fischhoff, 1982). A number of simple solutions have proven rather ineffective. It does not seem to help very much to exhort people to work harder, to raise the stakes hinging on their performance, to tell them about the problems that other people (like them) have with such tasks, or to provide theoretical knowledge of statistics or decision theory. Similarly, it does not seem reasonable to hope that the problems will go away with time or when the decisions are really important. Judgment is a skill that must be learned. Those who do not get training or who do not enjoy a naturally instructive environment (e.g., one that provides prompt unambiguous feedback and rewards people for wisdom rather than, say, for exuding confidence) will have difficulty going beyond the hard data at their disposal.

Although training courses in judgment per se are rare, many organized professions hope to inculcate good judgment as part of their apprenticeship program. This learning is expected to come about as a by-product of having one's behavior shaped by masters of the craft (be they architects, coaches, officers, or graduate advisers). What is learned is often hard to express in words and hence must be attributed to judgment (Polanyi, 1962). What is unclear is whether that learning extends to new decisions, for which the profession has not acquired trial-and-error experience to shape its practices.

When attempts have been made to improve judgment, a number of approaches have proven promising (Fischhoff, 1982). One is to provide the conditions that learning theory holds to be essential for skill acquisition; for example, whether forecasters show great skill in assessing the confidence to be placed in their precipitation forecasts—for which they receive prompt, pertinent, and unambiguous feedback that they are required to consider (Murphy and Winkler, 1984). It these conditions do not exist in life, then they might be simulated in the laboratory; for example, confidence assessment has been improved by giving concentrated training trials (Lichtenstein and Fischhoff, 1980). A second seemingly effective approach is to restructure how people perform judgment tasks, so as to enable them to use their own minds more effectively. For example, hindsight bias may be reduced by forcing people to imagine how events that did happen might not have happened (Slovic and Fischhoff, 1977); availability bias may be reduced by encouraging people to search their minds in a variety of ways so as to get a more diverse set of examples (Behn and Vaupel, 1983; Brown, Kahr, and Peterson, 1974; Keeney and Raiffa, 1976; Raiffa, 1968); new evidence may be interpreted more appropriately by having people consider how it might be consistent with hypotheses that they doubt (Fischhoff and Beyth-Marom, 1983; Kahneman and Tversky, 1979). Developing such procedures requires an understanding of how people do think as well as of how they should think. Finally, there is the obvious suggestion to train people in the principles of decision making, along with exercises in applying them to real problems. Researchers working in the area typically feel that they themselves have learned something from observing everyone else's problems. Whether this is an accurate perception and whether similar understanding can be conferred on others is an empirical question.

HOW IS DISTRIBUTED DECISION MAKING DIFFERENT?

If like is hard for single individuals wrestling with their fate, then what happens in command-and-control systems, with interdependent decision makers responsible for incompletely overlapping portions of complex problems? Addressing these situations is a logical next step for behavioral decision theory, although not one that it can take alone. Although the essential problem in command-and-control is still individuals pondering the unknown, there are now rigid machines, rules, and doctrines in the picture, along with more fluid social relations. These require the skills of computer scientists, human factors specialists, substantive experts, and organizational theorists.

What follows is our attempt to pull these perspectives together into a framework for analyzing command-and-control systems. In doing so, we have characterized the problem more generally as distributed decision making, defined as any situation in which decision-making information is not completely shared by those with a role in shaping the decision. The set of systems having this property includes high-tech examples, such as air traffic control and satellite management of a multinational corporation; mid-tech examples, such as forest fire fighting and police dispatch; low-tech examples, such as a volunteer organization's coordination of its branches' activities or a couple's integration of their childrearing practices or their use of a common checking account—as will as the command of a military operation or a far-flung foreign service.

We choose to look far afield for examples, in the belief that it is possible to understand one's own situation better by looking at the circumstances of others. They may do things so well or so poorly as to cast the viability of different strategies in sharp relief, as was the goal of *In Search of Excellence* (or might be the goal of its complement, *In Search of Dereliction*). Synthesizing the experience of diverse systems may highlight the significant dimensions in characterizing and designing other systems.

Although geographical separation is often considered a distinguishing characteristic of distributed decision making, there can be substantial difficulties in coordinating the (current and past) information of individuals in the same room or tent. (In the 1960s, some of these problems were called "failures to communicate.") As a result, we leave the importance of different kinds of separation as a matter for investigation. Although the distribution of decision-making authority might seem to be another distinguishing characteristic, we believe that it is trivially achieved in almost all human organizations. Few are able, even if they try, to centralize all authority to make decisions. It seems more productive to look at how decision-making authority is distributed. For example, even when there are focal decision makers who choose courses of action at clearly marked points in time, their choice is often refined through interactions with their subordinates, shaped by the information (and interpretations) reported by others, and constrained by the predecisions of their predecessors and superiors (e.g., avoid civilian casualties, avoid obviously reversing directions).

From this perspective, a useful unifying concept seems to be that of a *shared model.* Those living in distributed decision-making systems have to keep in mind some picture of many parts of that system, for example, how external forces are attempting to affect the system, what communications links exist within the system, what the different actors in the system believe about its internal and external situation, and what decisions they face (in terms of the options, values, constraints, and uncertainties). These beliefs are sometimes dignified by terms like *mental representation.* It seems unlikely than anyone (in our lifetimes, at least) will ever actually observe what goes on in people's minds with sufficient clarity to be able to outline the contents. What investigators can see is a refined and disciplined version of what other people can see, those aspects of people's beliefs that they are able to communicate. That communication might be in terms of unrestricted natural language, in terms of the restricted vocabulary of a formal organization, or in terms of a structured modeling language.

In all cases, though, people need to translate their thoughts into some language before those can be shared with others. Their ability to use the language sets an upper limit on the system's coordination of decision making, as does the system's procedures for information sharing. Looking at the language and procedures provides a way of characterizing a system's potential (and anticipating its problems). Looking at the knowledge that has been shared provides a way to characterize its current state of affairs (and anticipate its problems).

A reasonable question at this stage is why anyone should expect anything useful out of this effort or, indeed, why we should get into this topic rather than concentrate on more tractable problems. Command-and-control theory is a graveyard or good intentions. The stakes are so high that funders and fundees are willing to go with very long shots in hopes of producing some useful results. Yet the complexity of the problem is such that many of its theories appear almost autistic, as though the attempt to make sense of it leads researchers down a path to convoluted and idiosyncratic theorizing. Our hopes for beating these long odds lie in taking a fresh look at the problem, in bringing to it disciplinary perspectives that have not typically been combined (e.g., psychology, human factors, sociology, political science, as well as military science), in having experience with a variety of other distributed decision-making systems (e.g., public administration, technology management, finance, voluntary organizations), and in enjoying messy problems (which should keep us from reaching premature closure).

HOW DO DISTRIBUTED DECISION-MAKING SYSTEMS DIFFER?

At the core of distributed decision-making systems are the people who have to get the work done. As a result, a natural way to begin an analysis of such systems is with the reality faced by those individuals, wherever they find themselves within it. Sensible complications are to look, then, at the issues that arise when decision making is distributed over two individuals and, finally, when multiple individuals are involved.

The form of what follows is a *task analysis*, which is the standard point of entry for human factors engineers, the specialists concerned with the performance of people in technical systems. Such analyses characterize systems in terms of their behaviorally significant dimensions, which must be considered when designing the system and adapting people to it (Perrow, 1984). The substance of the present analysis follows most work on human factors in general, and its decision-making branch in particular, by emphasizing cognitive aspects of performance. It asks how people understand and manipulate their environment under reasonably unemotional conditions. Insofar as pressure and emotion degrade performance, problems that are unresolved at this level constitute a performance ceiling. For example, people need to stretch themselves to communicate at all. The risk that they may not stretch enough or in the right direction to be understood is part of the human condition. These risks can, however, be exacerbated (in predictable ways) by designers who do things such as compose multiservice task forces without making basic human communication and understanding a fundamental command concern.

Single-Person Systems

The simplest situation faced by an individual decision maker involves a static world about which everything can be known and no formal representation of knowledge is required. The threats to performance in this basic situation are those identified in the research on individual decision making (described above). They include the difficulties that arise in identifying relevant options, assembling and reviewing the knowledge that should be available, determining the values that are pertinent and the trade-offs among them, and integrating these pieces in an effective way. The aids to performance should also be those identified in the existing literature, such as checklists of options, multimethod value elicitation procedures, and integration help.[3]

A first complication for individual decision making is the addition of uncertainty. With it come all the difficulties of intuitive judgment under uncertainty, such as the misperception of causality, overconfidence in one's own knowledge, and heuristic-induced prediction biases. The potential solutions include training in judgmental skills, restructuring tasks so as to overcome bad habits, and keeping a statistical record of experience so as to reduce reliance on memory. A second complication is going from a static to a dynamic external world. With it come new difficulties, such as undue adherence to currently favored hypotheses, as well as the accompanying potential solutions, such as reporting forms that require consideration of how new evidence might be consistent with currently unfavored hypotheses. A third complication is use of a formal modeling language for organizing knowledge and decision making. One associated problem is the users'

[3]In the absence of a formal model, computational help is impossible. However, there are integration rules following other logics, such as flow charts, hierarchical lists of rules, or policy-capturing methods for determining what consistency with past decisions would dictate (Dawes, 1979; Goldberg, 1968; Meehl, 1954; Slovic, 1972).

inability to speak the modeling language; it might be addressed by using linguists or anthropologists to develop the language and train people in it. Another associated problem is the language's inability to describe certain situations (such as those including human factors or unclear intentions); it might be addressed by providing guidelines for overriding the conclusions produced from models using the language.

Two-Person Systems

Adding a second person to the system raises additional issues. However, before addressing them, it is important to ask what happens to the old issues. That is, are they eliminated, exacerbated, or left unchanged by the complications engendered by each kind of two-person system?

In behavioral terms, the simplest two-person system involves individuals with common goals, common experience, and a hardened communications link. Thus, they would have highly shared models and the opportunity to keep them consistent. Having a colleague can reduce some difficulties experienced by individuals. For example, information overload can be reduced by dividing information-processing responsibilities, and some mistakes can be avoided by having someone to check one's work. But having someone who thinks similarly in the system may just mean having two people prone to the same judgmental difficulties. It might even make matters worse if they drew confidence from the convergence of their (similarly flawed) judgmental processes.

More generally, agreement on any erroneous belief is likely to increase confidence without a corresponding increase in accuracy, perhaps encouraging more drastic (and more disastrous) actions. *Risky shift* is a term for groups' tendency to adopt more extreme positions than do their individual members (Davis, 1982; Myers and Lamm, 1976); *groupthink* is a term for the social processes that promote continued adherence to shared beliefs (Janis, 1972). Restricting communication would be one way to blunt these tendencies, however, at the price of allowing the models to drift apart, perhaps without the parties realizing it. Even with unrestricted communication, discrepant views can go a long while without being recognized. *False consensus* refers to the erroneous belief that others share one's views (Nisbett and Ross, 1980); *pluralistic ignorance* refers to the erroneous belief that one is the odd person out (Fiske and Taylor, 1984). Both have been repeatedly documented; both can be treated if the threat is recognized and facing the discrepancy is not too painful.

Such problems arise because frequency of interaction can create a perception of completely shared models, when sharing is inevitably incomplete. An obvious complication in two-person distributed decision-making systems is for experience to be obviously incomplete. Although this situation reduces the threat of unrecognized disagreement and increases the chances of erroneous beliefs' being challenged, it raises additional problems. One is the possibility that terms will unwittingly be used differently by the two, without the recognition that, say, *risk* or *threat* or *likely* or *destructive power* have different meanings (Beyth-Marom, 1982a, 1982b; Bunn and Tsipis, 1983; Fischhoff, Watson, and Hope, 1984). If such discrepancies go undetected, then the parties' perceptions will drift apart until some dramatic and unpredictable act occurs. To avoid having that happen at some inopportune time, inconsistencies must be actively sought and resolved (Beyth-Marom, 1982a, 1982b; Bunn and Tsipis, 1983; Fischhoff, Watson, and Hope, 1984; National Interagency Incident Management System, 1982). A contrasting problem is the inability to reconcile or even to face differences between models. When the differences are great enough to affect decisions, the skills of a mediator are needed to bring them together (Behm and Vaupel, 1983; Brown, Kahr, and Peterson, 1974; Keeney and Raiffa, 1976; Raiffa, 1968; von Winterfeldt and Edwards, 1982).

A common complication in two- (or multi-) person systems is unreliable communication links. Often this situation is imposed by external pressures, either directly (as when they attempt to disrupt communications) or indirectly (as when a hardened communication link is foregone to facilitate freedom of action within the team or to enhance the security of those communications that are made). Here, as elsewhere, the shared-models perspective suggests that this complication reduces some problems, raises others, and requires different systems design. For example, interrupting the communications links between individuals (or units) with deeply shared common experience allows them to acquire different information and formulate somewhat independent perspectives, thereby reducing the risk of groupthink. However, it may lead to unrecognized drift in their beliefs and unpredictable behavior when they are called to action. One possible protective device is to provide efficient checking procedures, enabling system members to detect and diagnose discrepancies in their models. The mixture of theoretical and empirical research needed to produce such procedures should also be able to produce general estimates of systems reliability, showing the level of vigilance appropriate for different circumstances.

One complication of concern for efficiency in communication is the imposition of institutional structures. These could include restricted vocabularies, time- or event-related reporting requirements, interaction protocols, or confirmation procedures ranging from repeating a message to deriving its implications. At the extreme, communication might be through an analytical language, designed to serve creation of the system's formal model of its world. The problems and possibilities of these languages for individual decision makers remain with multiple decision makers. An additional advantage that accrues from them is the ability to pool the knowledge of individuals with different experiences (e.g., observers on different fronts) in a single place. An additional disadvantage is that the language may suppress the nuances of normal communication that people depend on to understand and make themselves understood. It is unclear what substitutes people will find (or even if they will recognize the need to find them) when deprived of facial expression, body language, intonation, and similar cues. These problems may be further exacerbated when knowledge comes to reside in a model without indication of its source, so that model users do not know who said it, much less how it was said. Finally, models that cannot express the appropriate level of confidence for a subordinate's report probably cannot generate the confidence needed to follow a superior's choice of action—making it hard to lead through electronic mail.

The great memory capacity of automated aids makes it possible, in principle, to store such information. However, there are human problems both in getting and in presenting those additional cues. On the input side, one worries about people's inability to characterize the extent of their own knowledge, to translate it into the precise terms demanded by a language, or to see how they themselves relied on nonverbal cues to be understood. On the output side, one worries about creating meaningful displays of such qualifications. If shown routinely, they may clutter the picture with "soft" information which, in any case, gets lost when users attempt to integrate such uncertainties with best guesses at what is happening (Peterson, 1973). If available on request, qualifications may slip the minds of decision makers who want clear-cut answers to their questions. Because it is so difficult to tell when qualifications are not in order, such systems require careful design and their operators require careful training.[4] Unless users have demonstrated mastery of the system, it may be appropriate to sacrifice sophistication for fluency.[5]

A final, behaviorally significant complication that can arise with two-person distributed decision-making systems is inconsistencies in the goals of the parties. They may have similar values, but differ over the goals relevant to a particular case; they may have a common opponent, yet stand to share

[4]Samet (1975) showed that a commonly used military system required information to be characterized in terms of reliability and validity even though these concepts were not distinguished in the minds of users.

[5]A case to consider in this regard is the hot line between the United States and the Soviet Union. Although it might seem like a technical advance to upgrade the quality of the line so that the leaders could talk to one another directly (e.g., through videophone), perhaps the quality of the communication is better with the current telex systems with human operators who spend eight hours a day "talking" to one another. By contrast, given the differences between the cultures, who knows what unintentional cues would be sent by the leaders through their voices, postures, intonation, etc.?

differently from the spoils of victory; they may strive for power within the system, while still concerned about its ability to meet external challenges.[6] Like other complications, these can be useful. For example, disagreement over the application of general values can uncover labile values that might be undetected by an individual; competition might sharpen the wits of the competitors; by some accounts, conflict itself is part of what binds social units together (Coser, 1954). Moreover, the chances to address the liabilities of conflict are probably increased by how well they are known: working at cross purposes, distorting and withholding information, mistrust. Whether these chances are realized depends on how well those who design and operate such systems can identify and address the ways in which they are most vulnerable to competition. At times, this may mean introducing sharply defined reward systems to create the correct mix of incentives.[7]

Multiple-Person Systems

Most of the issues arising in the design and diagnosis of two-person systems also arise with multiple decision-maker systems, although with somewhat new wrinkles. The simplest level involves individuals with common goals, shared experience, and hardened communication links. As before, having more people around means having the opportunity for more views to evolve and be heard. Yet this advantage may backfire if the shared (past and present) experience leads them to think similarly while taking confidence in numbers (Lanir, 1982). As the number of parties multiplies, so does the volume of messages (and perhaps information). If hardened communications links mean that everyone hears everything, then there may be too much going on to ensure that everyone hears anything. More generally, it may be hard to keep track of who knows what. With an automated aid, it may be possible to reconstruct who heard what. With some modest modeling of the decision-making situations faced by different individuals, it may be possible to discern who needs to know what.

As organizational size increases, the possibility of completely shared experiences decreases. The maximum might be found in a hierarchical organization whose leaders had progressed through the ranks from the very bottom, so that they have a deep understanding of the reality of their subordinates' worlds, such that they can imagine what they might be

---

[6] A common variant within larger organizations is that they reward individuals within them for growth (i.e., making their own subunits larger), while striving as a whole for profit (Baumol, 1959).

[7] One example of the difficulty of diagnosing and designing such systems may be seen in the current debate over whether competition among the armed services improves national defense (by ensuring that there are technically qualified critics of each service's new weapons proposals) or degrades it (by fostering waste, duplication, and interoperability problems).

thinking and how they might respond in particular circumstances. In such situations, less needs to be said and more can be predicted, making the organization more intimate that it seems.

However, size also makes the liabilities of commonality more extreme. Not only is shared misunderstanding more likely, but it is also more difficult to treat because it is so broadly entrenched and the organizational climate is likely to be very rough for those who think differently. Indeed, the heterogeneity of an organization's selection and retention policies may be a good indicator of its resilience within a complex and changing reality. If there are any common biases in communications between individuals (e.g., underestimation of costs, exaggeration of expectations from subordinates), then the cumulative bias may be well out of hand by the time communications have cascaded up or down the organizational chart. When the world is changing rapidly, then the experience of having once been at every level in the organization may give an illusory feeling of understanding its reality. For example, the education, equipment, and challenges of foot soldiers (or sales representatives) may be quite different now than when their senior officers were in the trenches. An indicator of these threats might be the degree of technological change (or instability) in the organization and its environment. A treatment might be periodic rotation through the ranks and opportunities to cut through the normal lines of communication in order to find out what is really happening at diverse places, so as to reveal the discrepancies in the models held by different parties. Problems might be reduced somewhat by resisting opportunities to change the organization, unless the promised improvements will be so great as to compensate for the likely decrements in internal understanding.

Both the problems and promises of unshared experience increase as one goes from two- to multiperson systems. More people do bring more perspectives to a problem and with it the chances of challenging misconceptions. However, the intricacies of sharing and coordinating that information may become unmanageable. Even more seriously, with so many communication links, it may become nearly impossible even to discover the existence of misunderstandings, such as differences in unspoken assumptions or the usage of seemingly straightforward terms. If communications are decentralized, then various subunits may learn to speak to one another, solving their local problems but leaving the system as a whole unstable. If they are centralized, then the occupants of that controlling node have an opportunity to create a common picture, but doing so requires extraordinary attention to detail, regarding who believes what when and how they express those beliefs. One aid to tracking these complex realities is to maintain formal models of the decision-making problems faced at different places. Even if these models could capture only a portion of those situations, comparing the models held at headquarters and in the field might provide a structured way of focusing on discrepancies. When theory of data suggest that those discrepancies are large and persistent, then it may be command, rather than communications, strategies that require alteration. When leaders cannot understand their subordinates' world, one suggestion is to concentrate on telling them what to do, rather than how to do it, so as to avoid micromanagement that is unlikely to be realistic. A second is to recognize (and even solicit) signals suggesting that they, the leaders, are badly out of touch with their subordinates' perceptions (so that one or both sets of beliefs need adjustment).

Reliability problems in multiperson systems begin with those of two-person systems. As before, their cause may be external (e.g., disruptions, equipment failure) or internal (e.g., the desire for flexibility or autonomy). As before, the task of those in them is to discern when communications have failed, how they have failed (i.e., what messages have been interrupted or garbled), and how the system can be kept together. The multiplicity of communications means a greater need for a structured response, if the threat of unreliability is real and recognized. Depending on the organization's capabilities, one potential coping mechanism might be a communications protocol that emphasized staying in touch, even when there was nothing to say, in order to monitor reliability continually; another might be analyses of the backlash effect of actions or messages, considering how they discourage or restrict future communications (e.g., by suggesting the need for secrecy or revealing others' positions); another might be by reporting intentions along with current status, to facilitate projecting what incommunicant others might be doing; another might be creating a "black box" from which one could reconstruct what had happened before communications went down.

A complicating factor in reliability problems, which emerges here but could be treated with two-person systems, is that lost communications may reflect loss of the link or loss of the communicator at the other end of the link. That loss could reflect defection, disinterest, or destruction. Such losses simplify communications (by the number of links involving that individual) and can provide diagnostic information (about possible threats to the rest of the system). However, they require reformulation of all models within the system involving the lost individual. Where that reformulation cannot be confidently done or disseminated, then contingency plans are needed, expressing a best guess at how to act when the system may be shrinking. Whether drawn up for vanishing links or individuals, those plans should create realistic degrees of autonomy for making new decisions and for deviating from old ones (e.g., provide answers to: Are my orders still valid? Will I be punished for deviating from them?).

A final complicating factor with multiple-person systems, for which the two-person version exists but is relatively uninteresting, concerns the heterogeneity of its parts. At one extreme lies a homogeneous organization whose parts interact in an additive fashion, with each performing roughly the same functions and the system's strength depending on the sum of such parts. At the other extreme lies a heterogeneous organization having specialized parts dependent on one another for vital services, with its strength coming from the sophistication of its design and the effectiveness of its dedicated components. Crudely speaking, a large undifferentiated infantry group might anchor one end of this continuum and an integrated carrier strike force the other.

The operational benefits of a homogeneous system are its ability to use individuals and materials interchangeably, as well as its relative insensitivity to the loss of any particular units (insofar as their effect is additive). Common benefits as a distributed decision-making system are the existence of a shared organizational culture, the relative simplicity of organizational models, the ease with which components can interpret one another's actions, and the opportunity to create widely applicable organizational policies. Inherent limitations may include homogeneity of perspectives and skills, leaving the system relatively vulnerable to deeply shared misconceptions (what might be called "intellectual common-mode failures") and relatively devoid of the personnel resources need to initiate significant changes (or even detect the need for them without very strong, and perhaps painful, messages from the environment).

The operational benefits of a heterogeneous system lie in its ability to provide a precise response to any of the anticipated challenges posed by a complex environment. Its advantages as a distributed decision-making system lie in its ability to develop task-specific procedures, policies, and communications. One inherent disadvantage in this respect may be the difficulty of bearing in mind or modeling the operations of a complex interactive system, so it is hard to know who is doing what when and how their actions affect one another. For example, backlash and friendly fire may be more likely across diverse units than across similar ones. Even if they do have a clear picture of the whole, the managers of such a system may find it difficult to formulate an organizational philosophy with equivalent meanings in all the diverse contexts it faces. The diversity of parts may also create interoperability problems, hampering the parts' ability to communicate and cooperate amongst themselves.

Both kinds of systems may be most vulnerable to the kinds of threats against which the other is most strongly defended. The additive character of homogeneous systems means that it is numbers that count. A command system adapted to this reality may be relatively inattentive to those few ways in which individual units are indispensable, such as their ability to reveal vital organizational intelligence or to embarrass the organization as a whole. Conversely, the command structure that has evolved to orchestrate the pieces of a heterogeneous system may be severely challenged by situations in which mainly numbers matter. An inevitable by-product of specialization is having fewer of every specialty and less ability to transcend specialty boundaries. There may therefore be less staying power in protracted engagements.

Perhaps the best response to these limitations is incorporating some properties of each kind of system into the other. Thus, for example, homogeneous organizations could actively recruit individuals with diverse prior experience in order to ensure some heterogeneity of views; they might also develop specialist positions for dealing with nonadditive issues wherever those appear in the organization (e.g., intelligence officers, publishers' libel watchdogs). Heterogeneous organizations might promote generalists with the aim of mediating and attenuating the differences among their parts; they might also transfer specialists across branches so as to encourage the sharing of perspectives (at the price of their being less well equipped to do the particular job). Whether such steps are possible, given how antithetical they are to the ambient organizational philosophy, would be a critical design question.

PRINCIPLES IN DESIGNING DISTRIBUTED DECISION-MAKING SYSTEMS

Goals of the Analysis

The preceding task analysis began with the problems faced in designing the simplest of decision-making systems, those involving single individuals grappling with their fate under conditions of certainty, with no attempt at formalization. It proceeded to complicate the lives of those single individuals and then to consider several levels of complication within two-person and multiperson organizations. A full-blown version of this analysis would consider, at each stage, first, how the problems that arose in simpler systems were complicated or ameliorated and, second, what new problems arose. For each set of problems, it would try to develop a set of solutions based, as far as possible, on the available research literature in behavioral decision theory, cognitive psychology, human factors, communications research, or organizational theory. The recommendations offered here are therefore but speculations, suggestive of what would emerge from a fuller generic analysis or the consideration of specific systems.

That fuller analysis would proceed on two levels. One is to investigate solutions to highly specific problems, such as the communications protocol or optimal visual display for a particular heterogeneous system. The second is to develop general design principles, suggesting what to do in lieu of detailed specific studies. In reality, these two efforts are highly intertwined, with the general principles suggesting what behavioral dimensions merit detailed investigation and the empirical studies substantiating (or altering) those beliefs. Were a more comprehensive analysis in place, a logical extension would be to consider the interaction between two distributed decision-making systems, each characterized in the same general terms. Such an analysis might show how the imperfections of each might be exploited by the other as well as how they might lead to mutually undesirable circumstances. For example, an analysis of the National Command Authorities of the United States and the Soviet Union might show the kinds of challenges that each is least likely to handle effectively. That kind of diagnosis might serve as the basis for unilateral recommendations (or bilateral agreements) to the effect, "Don't test us in this way unless you really mean it. We're not equipped to respond flexibly."

Design Guidelines

Although still in its formative stages, the analysis to date suggests a number of general conclusions that might emerge from a more comprehensive analysis of distributed decision-making systems. One is that the design of the system needs to bear in mind the reality of the individuals at each node in it. If there is a tendency to let the design process be dominated by issues associated with the most recent complication, then it must be resisted. If the designers are unfamiliar with the world of the operators, then they must learn about it. For example, one should not become obsessed with the intricacies of displaying vast quantities of information when the real problem is not knowing what policy to apply. Given the difficulty of individual decision making, one must resist the temptation to move on to other, seemingly more tractable problems.

A second general conclusion is that many group problems may be seen as variants of individual problems or even as reflections of those problems not having been resolved. For example, a common crisis in the simplest individual decision-making situations is determining what the individual wants from them. The group analog is determining what specific policies to apply or how to interpret general policies in those circumstances. As another example, individuals' inability to deal coherently with uncertainty may underlie their (unrealistic) demands for certainty in communications from others.

A third conclusion is that many problems that are attributed to the imposition of novel technologies can be found in quite low-tech situations. Two people living in the same household can have difficulty communicating; allowing them to use only phone or telex may make matters better or worse. The speed of modern systems can induce enormous time pressures, yet many decisions cannot be made comfortably even with unlimited time. Telecommunications systems can generate information overload, yet the fundamental management problem remains the simple one of determining what is relevant. In such cases, the technology is best seen as giving the final form to problems that would have existed in any case and as providing a possible vehicle for either creating solutions or putting solutions out of reach.

A fourth conclusion is that is pays to accentuate the negative when evaluating the designs of distributed decision-making systems, and to accentuate the positive when adapting people to those systems. That is, the design of systems is typically a top-down process beginning with a set of objectives and normative constraints. The idealization that emerges is something for people to strive for but not necessarily something that they can achieve. Looking at how the system keeps people from doing their jobs provides more realistic expectations of overall system performance as well as focuses attention on where people need help. The point of departure for that help must be their current thought processes and capabilities, so that they can be brought along from where they are toward where one would like them to be. People can change, but only under carefully structured conditions and not that fast. When they are pushed too hard, then they risk losing touch with their own reality.

Design Ideologies

A fifth conclusion is that the design of distributed decision-making systems requires detailed empirical work. A condition for doing that work is resisting simplistic design philosophies. There is a variety of such principles, each having the kind of superficial appeal that is capable of generating strong organizational momentum, while frustrating efforts at more sensitive design. One such family of simple principles concentrates on dealing with a system's mistakes, by claiming to avoid them entirely in prospect (as expressed in "zero defects" or "quality is free" slogans), to adapt to them promptly in process (as expressed in "muddling through"), or to respond to them in hindsight ("learning from experience"). A second family concentrates on being ready for all contingencies, by instituting either rigid flexibility or rigid inflexibility, leaving all options open or planning for all contingencies. A third family emphasizes controlling the human element in systems, either by selecting the right people or by creating the right people (through proper training and incentives). A fourth family of principles proposes avoiding the human element either when it is convenient (because viable alternatives exist), when it is desirable (because humans have known flaws), or in all possible circumstances whether or not human fallibility has been demonstrated (in hopes of increasing system predictability).

Rigid subscription to any of these principles gives the designers (and operators) of a system an impossible task. For example, the instruction "to avoid all errors" implies that time and price are unimportant. When this is not the case, the designers are left adrift, forced to make trade-offs without explicit guidance. When fault-free design is impossible, then the principle discourages treatment of those faults that do remain. Many fail-safe systems work only because the people in them have learned, by trial and error, to diagnose and respond to problems that are not supposed to happen. Because the existence of such unofficial intelligence has no place in the official design of the system, it may have to be hidden, may be unable to get needed resources (e.g., for record keeping or realistic exercises), and may be destroyed by any uncontrollable change in the system (which invalidates operators' understanding of those intricacies of its operation that do not appear in any plans or training manuals). From this perspective, when perfection is impossible, it may be advisable to abandon near-perfection as a goal as well, so as to ensure that there are enough problems for people to learn to cope with them. In addition, when perfection is still (but) an aspiration, steps toward it should be very large before they justify disrupting accustomed (unwritten) relationships. That is, technological instability is a threat to system operation. Additional threats of this philosophy include unwillingness to face those intractable problems that do remain and setting the operators up to take the rap when their use of the system proves impossible.

Similar analyses exist for the limitations of each of the other simple rules. In response, proponents might say that the rules are not meant to be taken literally and that compromises are a necessary part of all design. Yet the categorical nature of such principles is an important part of their appeal and, as stated, they provide no guidance or legitimation for compromises. Moreover, they often tend to embody a deep misunderstanding of the role of people in person-machine systems, reflecting, in one way or another, a belief in the possibility of engineering the human side of the operation in the way that one might hope to engineer the mechnical or electronics side.

Human Factors

As the long list of human factors failures in technical systems suggests, the attempts to implement this belief are often needlessly clumsy (National Research Council, 1983; Perrow, 1984; Rasmussen and Rouse, 1981). The extensive body of human factors research is either unknown or is invoked at such a late stage in the design process that it can amount to little more than the development of warning labels and training programs for coping with inhuman systems. It is so easy to speculate about human behavior (and provide supporting anecdotal evidence) that systematic empirical research hardly seems needed. Common concomitants of insensitive design are situations in which the designers (or those who manage them) have radically different personal experiences from the operators, themselves work in organizations that do not function very well interpersonally, or are frustrated in trying to understand why some group of others (e.g., the public) does not like them.

However, even when the engineering of people is sensitive, its ambitions are often misconceived. The complexity of systems places some limits on their perfectability, making it hard to understand the intricacies of a design. As a result, one can neither anticipate all problems nor confidently treat those one can anticipate, without the fear that corrections made in one domain will create new problems in another.[8] Part of the genius of people is their ability to see (and hence respond to) situations in unique (and hence unpredictable) ways. Although this creativity can be seen in even the most structured psychomotor tasks, it is central and inescapble in any interesting distributed decision-making system (Fischhoff, Lanir, and Johnson, in press). Once people have to do any real thinking, the system becomes complex (and hence unperfectable). In such cases, the task of engineering is to help the operators understand the system, rather than to manage them as part of it. A common sign of insensitivity in this regard is use of the term *operator error* to describe problems arising from the interaction of operator and system. A sign of sensitivity is incorporating operators in the design process. A rule of thumb is that human problems seldom have purely technical solutions, while technical solutions typically create human problems (Reason, in press).

THE POSSIBILITY OF DISTRIBUTED DECISION MAKING

Pursuing this line of inquiry can point to specific problems arising in destributed decision-making systems and focus technical efforts on solving them. Those solutions might include displays for uncertain information, protocols for communication in complex systems, training programs for making do with unfriendly systems, contingency plans for coping with predictable system failures, and terminology for coordinating diverse units. Deriving such solutions is technically difficult, but part of a known craft.

---

[8]The nuclear industry's attempts to deal with the human factors problems identified at Three Mile Island provide a number of clear examples. To take but two: (a) increasing the number of potentially dangerous situations in which it is necessary to shut down a reactor has increased the frequency with which reactors are in transitory states in which they are less well controlled and in which their components are subject to greater stresses (thereby reducing their life expectancy by some poorly understood amount); (b) increasing the number of human factors-related regulations has complicated operators' jobs at the plant and created lucrative opportunities for operators to work as consultants to industry (thereby reducing the qualified labor force at the plants).

Investigators know how to describe such problems, devise possible remedies, and subject those remedies to empirical test. When the opportunities to develop solutions are limited, these kinds of perspectives can help characterize existing systems and improvise balanced responses to them.

However, although these solutions might make systems better, they cannot make them whole. The pursuit of them may even pose a threat to systems design if it distracts attention from the broader question of how systems are created and conceptualized. In both design and operation, healthy systems enjoy a creative tension between various conflicting pressures. One is between a top-down perspective (working down toward reality from an idealization of how the system should operate) and a bottom-up perspective (working up from reality toward some modest improvement of the current presenting symptoms). Another is between bureaucratization and innovation (or inflexibility and flexibility). Yet others are between planning and reacting, between a stress on routine and crisis operations, between risk acceptance and risk aversion, between human and technology orientation. A common thread in these contrasts is the system's attitude toward uncertainty: Does it accept that as a fact of life or does it live in the future, oriented toward the day when everything is predictable or controllable?

Achieving a balance between these perspectives requires both the insight needed to be candid about the limitations of one's system and the leadership needed to withstand whichever pressures dominate at the moment. When a (dynamic) balance is reached, the system can use its personnel most effectively and develop realistic strategies. When it is not reached, the organization is in a state of crisis, vulnerable to events or to hostile actions that exploit its imbalances. The crisis is particularly great when the need for balance is not recognized or cannot be admitted (within the current organizational culture), and when an experimental gulf separates management and operators. In this light, one can tell a great deal about how a system functions by looking at its managers' philosophy. If that is oversimplified or overconfident, then the system will be too, despite any superficial complexity. The goal of a task analysis then becomes to expose the precise ways in which this vulnerability expresses itself.

REFERENCES

Armstrong, J.S.
1985 *Long-range forecasting*. Second edition. New York: Wiley.

Bailey, R.W.
1982 *Human Performance in Engineering*. Englewood Cliffs, NJ: Prentice Hall.

Bar Hillel, M.
1980 The base-rate fallacy in probability judgments. *Acta Psychologica* 44:211-233.

1984 Representativeness and fallacies of probability judgment. *Acta Psychologica* 55:91-107.

Baumol, W.J.

1959 *Business Behavior, Value and Growth.* New York: Macmillam.

Beach, L.R., and Mitchell, T.R.

1978 A contingency model for the selection of decision strategies. *Academy of Management Review* 3:439-449.

Beach L.R., Townes, B.D., Campbell, F.L., and Keating, G.W.

1976 Developing and testing a decision aid for birth planning decisions. *Organizational Behavior and Human Performance* 15:99-116.

Behn, R.D., and Vaupel, J.W.

1983 *Quick Analysis for Busy Decision Makers.* New York: Basic Books.

Berkeley, D., and Humphreys, P.C.

1982 Structuring decision problems and the "bias heuristic." *Acta Psychologica* 50:201-252.

Behth-Marom, R.

1982a How probable is probable? Numerical translation of verbal probability expressions. *Journal of Forecasting* 1:257-269.

1982b Perception of correlation reexamined. *Memory and Cognition* 10:511-519.

Beyth-Marom, R., Dekel, S., Gombo, R. and Shaked, M.

1985 *An Elementary Approach to Thinking Under Uncertainty.* Hillscale, NY: Erlbaum.

Brehmer, B.

1980 Effect of cue validity on learning of complex rules in probabilistic inference tasks. *Acta Psychologica* 44:201-210.

Brown, R.V., Kahr, A.S., and Peterson, C.

1974 *Decision Analysis for the Manager.* New York: Holt, Rinehart and Winston.

Bunn, M., and Tsipis, K.

1983 The uncertainties of preemptive nuclear attack. *Scientific American* 249(5): 38-47.

Corbin, R.

1980 On decisions that might not get made. In T. Wallsten, ed., *Cognitive Processes in Choice and Decision Processes.* Hillsdale, NJ: Erlbaum.

Coser, L.A.

1954 *The Social Functions of Conflict.* Glencoe, IL: The Free Press.

Davis, J.H.

1982 *Group Performance.* Reading, MA: Addison-Wesley.

Dawes, R.M.

1979 The robust beauty of improper linear models in decision making. *American Psychologist* 34:571-582.

Edwards, W

1954 The theory of decision making. *Psychological Bulletin* 51:201-214.

1961 Behavioral decision theory. *Annual Review of Psychology* 12:473-498.

Einhorn, H.J., and Hogarth, R.M.

1978 Confidence in judgment: Persistence in the illusion of validity. *Psychological Review* 85:395-416.

1981 Behavioral decision theory: Processes of judgment and choice. *Annual Review of Psychology* 32:53-88.

Ericsson, A., and Simon, H.

1980 Verbal reports as data. *Psychological Review* 87:215-251.

Feather, N., ed.

1982 *Expectancy, Incentive and Action*. Hillsdale, NJ: Erlbaum.

Fischhoff, B.

1975 Hindsight≠foresight: The effect of outcome knowledge on judgment under uncertainty. *Journal of Experimental Psychology: Human Perception and Performance* 1:288-299.

1980 Clinical decision analysis. *Operations Research* 28:28-43.

1982 Debiasing. In D. Kahneman, P. Slovic, and A. Tversky, eds., *Judgment Under Uncertainty: Heuristics and Biases*. New York: Cambridge University Press.

1984 Setting standards: A systematic approach to managing public health and safety risks. *Management Science* 30:834-843.

1987 Judgment and decision making. In R. Sternberg and E.E. Smith, eds., *The Psychology of Thinking*. New York: Cambridge University Press.

1988 Eliciting expert judgment. *IEEE Transactions on Systems, Man, and Cybernetics* 13:448-661.

Fischhoff, B., and Beyth-Marom, R.

1983 Hypothesis evaluation from a Bayesian perspective. *Psychological Review* 90:239-260.

Fischhoff, B., and Cox, L.A., Jr.

1985 Conceptual framework for benefit assessment. In J.D. Bentkover, V.T. Covello, and J. Mumpower, eds., *Benefits Assessment: The State of the Art*. Dordrecht, The Netherlands: D. Reidel.

Fischhoff, B., Lanir, Z., and Johnson, S.

in press Risky lessons: A framework for analyzing attempts to learn in organizations. *Organization Science*.

Fischhoff, B., Slovic, P., and Lichtenstein, S.

1978 Fault trees: Sensitivity of estimated failure probabilities to problem representation. *Journal of Experimental Psychology: Human Perception and Performance* 4:330-344.

1980 Knowing what you want: Measuring labile values. In T. Wallsten, ed., *Cognitive Processes in Choice and Decision Behavior*. Hillsdale, NJ: Erlbaum.

Fischhoff, B., Svenson, O., and Slovic, P.

1987 Active responses to environmental hazards. In D. Stokols and I. Altman, eds., *Handbook of Environmental Psychology*. New York: Wiley.

Fischhoff, B., Watson, S., and Hope, C.

1984 Defining risk. *Policy Sciences* 17:123-139.

Fiske, S., and Taylor, S.E.

1984 *Social Cognition*. Reading, MA: Addison Wesley.

Gettys, C.F., Pliske, R.M., Manning, C., and Casey, J.T.

1987 An evaluation of human act gereration performance. *Organizational Behavior and Human Decision Processes* 39:23-51.

Goldberg, L.R.

1968 Simple models or simple processes? Some research on clinical judgments. *American Psychologist* 23:483-496.

Grether, D.M., and Plott, C.R.

1979 Economic theory of choice and the preference reversal phenomenon. *American Economic Review* 69:623-638.

Hammer, W.

1980 *Product Safety and Management Engineering*. Englewood Cliffs, NJ: Prentice-Hall.

Hechter, M., Cooper, L., and Nadel, L., eds.
in press *Values*. Stanford, Calif.: Stanford University Press.

Hershey, J.C., Kunreuther, H.C., and Schoemaker, P.J.H.
1982 Sources of bias in assessment procedures for utility functions. *Management Science* 28:936-954.

Hogarth, R.M.
1982 Beyond discrete biases: Functional and dysfunctional aspects of judgmental heuristics. *Psychological Bulletin* 90:197-217.

Humphreys, P., Svenson, O., and Vari, A., eds.,
1983 *Analyzing and Aiding Decision Processes*. Amsterdam: North Holland.

Janis, I.L.
1972 *Victims of Groupthink*. Boston: Houghton Mifflin.
1982 *Counseling on Personal Decisions*. New Haven: Yale University Press.

Janis, I.L., and Mann, L.
1977 *Decision Making*. New York: Free Press.

Jungermann, H.
1984 The two camps on rationality. In R.W. Scholz, ed., *Decision Making Under Uncertainty*. Amsterdam: Elsevier.

Kahneman, D., and Tversky, A.
1972 Subjective probability: A judgment of representativeness. *Cognitive Psychology* 3:430-454.
1979 Prospect theory. *Econometrics* 47:263-292.

Kahneman, D., Slovic, P., and Tversky, A.
1982 *Judgment Under Uncertainty: Heuristics and Biases*. New York: Cambridge University Press.

Keeney, R.L., and Raiffa, H.
1976 *Decisions With Multiple Objectives: Preferences and Value Tradeoffs*. New York: Wiley.

Kidd, J.B.
1970 The utilization of subjective probabilities in production planning. *Acta Psychologica* 34:338-347.

Koriat, A., Lichtenstein, S., and Fischhoff, B.
1980 Reasons for confidence. *Journal of Experimental Psychology: Human Learning and Memory* 6:107-118.

Lanir, T.
1982 *Strategic Surprises*. Ramat Aviv: Tel Aviv University Press.

Lichtenstein, S., and Fischhoff, B.
1980 Training for calibration. *Organizational Behavior and Human Performance* 26:149-171.

Lichtenstein, S., Fischhoff, B., and Phillips, L.D.
1982 Calibration of probabilities: State of the art to 1980. In D. Kahneman, P. Slovic, and A., Tversky, eds., *Judgment Under Uncertainty: Heuristics and Biases*. New York: Cambridge University Press.

Lichtenstein, S., Slovic, P., and Zink, D.
1969 Effect of instruction in expected value on optimality of gambling decisions. *Journal of Experimental Psychology* 79:236-240.

March, J.G.
1978 Bounded rationality, ambiguity, and the engineering of choice. *The Bell Journal of Economics* 9:587-608.

McCormick, N.J.
1981 *Reliability and Risk Analysis*. New York: Academic Press.

Meehl, P.E.
1954 *Clinical vs. Statistical Prediction: A Theoretical Analysis and a Review of the Evidence*. Minneapolis: University of Minnesota Press.
Miller, G.A.
1956 The magical number seven, plus or minus two: Some limits on our capacity for processing information. *Psychological Review* 63:81-97.
Mischel, W.
1968 *Personality and Assessment*. New York: Wiley.
Montgomery, H.
1983 Decision rules and the search for a dominance structure: Towards a process model of decision making. In P. Humphreys, O. Svenson, and A. Vari, eds., *Analyzing and Aiding Decision Processes*. Amsterdam: North Holland.
Murphy, A.H., and Winkler, R.L.
1984 Probability of precipitation forecasts. *Journal of the American Statistical Association* 79:391-400.
Myers, D.G. and Lamm, H.
1976 The group polarization phenomenon. *Psychological Bulletin* 83(4):602-627.
National Interagency Incident Management System
1982 *The What, Why, and How of NIIMS*. Washington, DC: U.S. Dept. of Agriculture.
National Research Council.
1981 *Surveys of Subjective Phenomena*. Committee on National Statistics. Washington DC: National Academy Press.
1983 *Research Needs in Human Factors*. Committee on Human Factors. Washington, DC: National Academy Press.
Nisbett, R.E., and Ross, L.
1980 *Human Inference: Strategies and Shortcomings of Social Judgment*. Englewood Cliffs, NJ: Prentice-Hall.
Nisbett, R.E., and Wilson, T.D.
1977 Telling more than we can know: Verbal reports on mental processes. *Psychological Review* 84:231-259.
Payne, J.W.
1982 Contingent decision behavior. *Psychological Bulletin* 92:382-401.
Perrow, C.
1984 Normal Accidents. New York: Basic Books.
Peterson, C.R., and Beach, L.R.
1967 Man as an intuitive statistician. *Psychological Bulletin* 63:29-46.
Peterson, C.R., ed.
1973 Special issue: Cascaded inference. *Organizational Behavior and Human Performance* 10:310-432.
Pitz, G.S., and Sachs, N.J.
1984 Behavioral decision theory. *Annual Review of Psychology* 35.
Pitz, G.F., Sachs, N.J., and Heerboth, J.
1980 Procedures for eliciting choices in the analysis of individual decisions. *Organizational Behavior and Human Performance* 26:396-408.
Polanyi, M.
1962 *Personal Knowledge*. London: Routledge and Kegan Paul.
Raiffa, H.
1968 *Decision Analysis*. Reading, MA: Addison-Wesley.
Rappoport, A., and Wallsten, J.S.
1972 Individual decision behavior. *Annual Review of Psychology* 23:131-175.

Rasmussen, J., and Rouse, W.B., eds.
1981 *Human Detection and Diagnosis of System Failure*. New York: Plenum.

Reason
in press *Human Error*. New York: Cambridge University Press.

Rokeach, M.
1973 *The Nature of Human Values*. New York: The Free Press.

Ross, L.
1977 The intuitive psychologist and his shortcomings: distortions in the attribution process. Pp. 174-177 in L. Berkowitz, ed., *Advances in Experimental Social Psychology* (Vol. 10). New York: Academic Press.

Samet, M.G.
1975 Quantitative interpretation of two qualitative scales used to rate military intelligence. *Human Factors* 17:192-202.

Schoemaker, P.J.H.
1983 The expected utility model: Its variants, purposes, evidence and limitations. *Journal of Economic Literature* 20:528-563.

Shaklee, H., and Mimms, M.
1982 Sources of error in judging event covariations: Effects of memory demands. *Journal of Experimental Psychology: Learning, Memory, and Cognition* 8:208-224.

Shaklee, H., and Tucker, D.
1980 A rule analysis of judgments of covariation events. *Memory and Cognition* 8:459-467.

Simon, H.
1957 *Models of Man: Social and Rational*. New York: Wiley.

Slovic, P.
1972 Psychological study of human judgment: Implications for investment decision making. *Journal of Finance* 27:779-799.

Slovic, P., and Fischhoff, B.
1977 On the psychology of experimental surprises. *Journal of Experimental Psychology: Human Perception and Performance* 3:1-39.

Slovic, P., Fischhoff, B., and Lichtenstein, S.
1977 Behavioral decision theory. *Annual Review of Psychology* 28, 1-39.

Slovic, P., and Lichtenstein, S.
1983 Preference reversals: A broader perspective. *American Economic Review* 73:596-605.

Slovic, P., Lichtenstein, S., and Fischhoff, B.
1988 Decision making. In R.C. Atkinson, R.J. Hernstein, G. Lindzey, and R.D. Luce, eds., *Stevens' Handbook of Experimental Psychology* (second edition). New York: Wiley.

Slovic, P., and Tversky, A.
1974 Who accepts Savage's axiom? *Behavioral Science* 19:368-373.

Stokey, E., and Zeckhauser, R.
1978 *A Primer for Policy Analysis*. New York: Norton.

Svenson, O.
1981 Are we all less risky and more skillful than our fellow drivers? *Acta Psychologica* 47:143-148.

Tihansky, D.
1976 Confidence assessment of military air frame cost predictions. *Operations Research* 24:26-43.

Tversky, A.
1969 Intransitivity of preferences. *Psychological Review* 76:31-48.
Tversky, A., and Kahneman, D.
1973 Availability: A heuristic for judging frequency and probability. *Cognitive Psychology* 4:207-232.
1981 The framing of decisions and the psychology of choice. *Science* 211:453-458.
U.S. Nuclear Regulatory Commission
1983 *PRA Procedures Guide* (NUREG/CR-2300). Washington, DC: The Commission.
von Winterfeldt, D., and Edwards, W.
1982 Costs and payoffs in perceptual research. *Psychological Bulletin* 93:609-622.
1986 *Decision Making and Behavioral Research*. New York: Cambridge University Press.
Wagenaar, W., and Sagaria, S.
1976 Misperception of experimental growth. *Perception and Psychophysics*.
Wallsten, T., and Budescu, D.
1983 Encoding subjective probabilities: A psychological and psychometric review. *Management Science* 29:151-173.
Weinstein, N.D.
1980 Unrealistic optimism about future life events. *Journal of Personality and Social Psychology* 39:806-820.
Wheeler, D.D., and Janis, I.L.
1980 *A Practical Guide for Making Decisions*. New York: The Free Press.
Wilson, R., and Crouch, E.
1982 *Risk/Benefit Analysis*. Cambridge, MA: Ballinger.
Yates, J.F.
1989 *Judgment and Decision Making*. Chichester, Eng.: Wiley.

Appendix B
Background Materials

Carley, Kathleen M.

1986a An approach for relating social structure to cognitive structure. *Journal of Mathematical Sociology* 12(2):137-189.

1986b Knowledge acquisition as a social phenomenon. *Instructional Science* 13:381-438.

1986c Separating the Effects of Structure and Interaction. Working paper. Carnegie Mellon University.

1987 Frame-based Decision Making in a Distributed Decision-Making Environment. Working paper. Carnegie Mellon University.

1988 Distributed information and organizational decision-making models. Andrew Sage, ed., *Concise Encyclopedia of Information Processing in Systems and Organizations*. New York: Pergamon Press.

1986 Distributed Decision Making. Working paper. Carnegie Mellon University.

Charny, Leonid, and T.B. Sheridan

1986 Satisfying Decision Making in Supervisory Control. Working paper. Massachusetts Institute of Technology, Man-Machine Systems Laboratory.

Coombs, Clyde H.

1986 Some Views on Distributed Decision Making. Working paper. University of Michigan.

Dawes, Robyn M.

1986 Distributed Decision Making: Position Paper. Working paper. Carnegie Mellon University.

Disney, Ralph L.

1986 Some Comments on Distributed Decision Systems. Working paper. Virginia Polytechnic Institute and State University.

Disney, Ralph L., and D. Konig

1985 Queueing networks: A survey of their random processes. *Society for Industrial and Applied Mathematics* 27(3):335-403.

Grusky, Oscar

1986 Comments on the Fischhoff-Johnson Model of Distributed Decision Making. University of California, Los Angeles.

Hirschhorn, Larry

1986a The Cognitive-Emotional Domain: Comments on Fischhoff-Johnson Paper. Working paper. Wharton School of the University of Pennsylvania.

1986b Research Directions for Members of the Human Factors Community Concerned With Nuclear Reactor Safety: Perspectives From the Field of Organization Design. Working paper. Wharton School of the University of Pennsylvania.

Hurd, R.W., and J.K. Kriesky

1986 Communications. *Industrial and Labor Relations Review* 40(1):115-122.

Klein, Gary A.

1986 *Analogical Decision Making*. Interim Report MDA903-85-C-0327, prepared for Army Research Institute for the Behavioral and Social Sciences. Klein Associates: Yellow Springs, Ohio.

Klein, Gary A., R. Calderwood, and A. Clinton-Cirocco

1986 Rapid decision making on the fire ground. *Proceedings of the Human Factors Society 30th Annual Meeting*. Santa Monica, Calif.: Human Factors Society.

LaPorte, Todd R.

1984 Technology as Social Organization. Working paper No. 84-1. Institute of Governmental Studies, University of California, Berkeley.

1986 Distributed Decision Making and High Reliability Organizations. Working paper 86-3. Institute of Governmental Studies, University of California, Berkeley.

Lewin, Arie

1986 Organizational Design: A Historic Synthesis and the Challenges for Future Research. Paper presented at meeting of the Academy of Management, Chicago, Ill.

March, J.G., and J.P. Olsen

1984 The new institutionalism: Organizational factors in political life. *American Political Science Review* 78(3):734-749.

March, J.G., and R. Weissinger-Baylon, eds.

1986 *Ambiguity and Command: Organizational Perspectives on Military Decision Making*. Boston, Mass.: Pitman.

Mendel, Max B., and T.B. Sheridan

1986 *Optimal Combination of Information From Multiple Sources*. Cambridge, Mass.: Massachusetts Institute of Technology, Man-Machine Systems Laboratory.

Moore, Molly

1986 U.S. troops find weapons too complex. *The Washington Post*, pp. 1, 8-9.

Morris, James H., M. Satyanarayanan, M.H. Conner, J.H. Howard, D.S.H. Rosenthal, and F.D. Smith

1986 Andrew: A distributed personal computing environment. *Communications of the ACM* 29(3):184-201.

Northrup, Herbert R.

1986 The rise and demise of PATCO. *Industrial and Labor Relations Review* 40(1):122-128.

Pate-Cornell, M.E.

1984 Fault trees vs. event trees in reliability analysis. *Risk Analysis* 4(3):177-186.

1986 Warning systems in risk management. *Risk Analysis* 6(2):223-234.

Pate-Cornell, M.E., and J.E. Neu

1985 Warning systems and defense policy. *Risk Analysis* 5(2):121-128.

Presidential Commission on the Space Shuttle Challenger Accident

1986 *Report of the Presidential Commission on the Space Shuttle Challenger Accident.* Washington, D.C.: U.S. Government Printing Office.

Rochlin, Gene I., T.R. LaPorte, and K.H. Roberts

1987 The self-designing high-reliability organization: Aircraft carrier flight operations at sea. *Naval War College Review* (Autumn):76-90.

Roseborough, James B., and T.B. Sheridan

1986 *Aiding Human Operators With State Estimates.* Cambridge, Mass.: Massachusetts Institute of Technology, Man-Machine Systems Laboratory.

Sheridan, Thomas B., L. Charny, M. Leonid, M.B. Mendel, and J.B. Roseborough

1986 *Supervisory Control, Mental Models and Decision Aids.* Cambridge, Mass.: Massachusetts Institute of Technology, Man-Machine Systems Laboratory.

Thompson, Frederick D.

No date *An Operations Analysis Perspective on Distributed Decision Making.* Alexandria, Va.: Center for Naval Analysis.

1983 *Beyond the War Game Mystique.* Proceedings of the United States Naval Institute.

Williamson, Oliver E.

1981 The economics of organization: The transaction cost approach. *American Journal of Sociology* 87(3):548-574.

Williamson, Oliver E.

1986 Distributed Decision Making: Applications Of The Transaction Cost Economics Perspective. Working Paper. Yale University, Department of Economics.